WHAT PEOPLE

THE INTE(

As Dr. Kavar has done so well in his previous writing, he's created a really thoughtful conversation around how we integrate our spirituality and our clinical work. Having known Lou for a few years now, I "hear" his voice as he communicates his thoughtful insights about the integration of self and practice. As he embraces his own empirical nature, he talks clearly and effectively about the "methodology" of spiritual assessment. I believe clinicians, clergy, and practitioners of pastoral care can benefit from reading this insightful and thoughtful book!
Dr. Wm. David Chapman, Psy.D., Dean, Harold Able School of Social and Behavioral Sciences, Capella University, Minneapolis, MN

Dr. Kavar makes the often obscure language of spirituality accessible to the clinician and the students who strive to become clinicians. His premise that spirituality is an integral dimension of self allows mental health providers a way to help clients recognize, validate, and cultivate true body-mind-spirit unity. This book is truly remarkable.
Sally Dodds, MSW, Ph.D., Associate Professor/Research Scholar of Medicine, University of Arizona Center for Integrative Medicine

The Integrated Self provides a wonderful blueprint for realizing spiritual life in counseling whether within a sacred tradition or not. Lou blends theory with practice seamlessly weaving together a holistic approach to a difficult and often controversial subject in therapeutic practice. A must read whether you are a practicing psychologist, chaplain or pastor!
Dr. Thomas C. Vail, United States Military Chaplain.

Dr. Kavar has written a scholarly guide that is grounded in research, yet, accessible to everyone seeking spiritual integration in their lives – and isn't that all of us? The Integrated Self is cutting edge in this growing field of spiritual awareness and a must-read for all who are at a point of consciously trying to grow in their lives. This book can open a door.

Kathleen M. Kowalski Trakofler, Ph.D. Research Psychologist, National Institute of Occupational Safety and Health, Centers for Disease Control, Department of Health and Human Services (USA)

As a psychologist who works in sport, you often work with athletes at a time when they are making themselves vulnerable and stepping outside of their comfort zone. Sport psychology professionals frequently talk with athletes about the importance of who they are and bringing themselves to what they do. Spirituality is one piece of who that athlete is, and for some athletes it may be a source of strength. This book provides a model that can be beneficial for those psychologists wishing to begin exploring spirituality with athletes, and may be helpful to those wishing to incorporate this into their practice.

Dr. Adrienne Leslie-Toogood, Psychologist, Canadian Sport Centre Manitoba

The Integrated Self presents a ground-breaking way of approaching client's that considers the core of the person, including culture and spirituality. His approach is insightful and unlike approaches in social work today.

Michelle Chan, MSW, Registered Social Worker, Hong Kong, China

The Integrated Self:

A Holistic Approach to Spirituality and Mental Health Practice

The Integrated Self:

A Holistic Approach to Spirituality and Mental Health Practice

Louis F. Kavar, Ph.D.

BOOKS

Winchester, UK
Washington, USA

First published by O-Books, 2012
O-Books is an imprint of John Hunt Publishing Ltd., Laurel House, Station Approach,
Alresford, Hants, SO24 9JH, UK
office1@o-books.net
www.o-books.com

For distributor details and how to order please visit the 'Ordering' section on our website.

Text copyright: Louis F. Kavar 2011

ISBN: 978 1 84694 904 3

A CIP catalogue record for this book is available from the British Library.

Design: Stuart Davies

Printed in the UK by CPI Antony Rowe
Printed in the USA by Offset Paperback Mfrs, Inc

We operate a distinctive and ethical publishing philosophy in all
areas of our business, from our global network of authors to
production and worldwide distribution.

CONTENTS

Dedication

In thanksgiving for the gentle and quiet life of
Dr. Richard Byrne, OCSO, whose death from complications due
to AIDS was marked by isolation and fear.
May the memory of his life inspire compassion among others.

Acknowledgements

In gratitude to:

Alicia von Stamwitz, whose expertise was invaluable in the development of the manuscript for this book;

Alan Eddington, whose keen eye and thoughtful analysis added to the quality of this book through proof reading and discussion;

And most especially my beloved, Chi Kin Lo, whose support of my work has brought it to greater fruition.

In appreciation to John Hunt and the staff at O-Books for their expertise and pursuit of excellence in publishing.

Introduction

It happened more than thirty years ago. Confused by a series of difficult life events, some of which included her father's passing and financial concerns, she remembers a day trip to a state park to go hiking. After climbing up a ridge, she sat on a rock and looked over the vista. "I can't tell you exactly what happened. But something came over me and I knew it would be okay." As she describes the experience, tears begin to well in her eyes and her choice of words become more deliberate. "Nothing in my life had really changed, but from that point on, I had a sense of peace. I knew it would all be okay. Here I am now in my fifties and I know, it has been more than just okay."

As clinicians, we have witnessed it many times. People tell us stories of transformative moments in their lives and we witness the same phenomenon. There are noticeable changes in their affect. The pace of speech slows and becomes more deliberate. Words are chosen carefully. It becomes clear that the words do not fully capture the experience. Emotion that was felt in the original experience, often twenty or thirty years before the telling of the story, is fresh and felt once again.

The woman who shared this story was asked to share an event in her life that she would consider spiritual. She was told that it could be anything, but to focus on one particular event or experience. As different as such experiences are from one person to another, these stories convey potency about the experiences. In these spiritual experiences, the individual discovers some kind of clarity or focus that did not previously exist.

In the practice of psychology today, strength-based models of treatment that invite the client to build on existing strengths in addressing particular behavioral or emotional problems are commonly used by clinicians. In strength-based models of treatment, a client's resiliency becomes a critical factor for positive treatment outcomes.

The spiritual experience described by the woman in this illustration demonstrates that there is something about the experience itself that provided resiliency in a difficult time of life. The resiliency drawn from the experience enabled her to mobilize strength far greater than therapeutic techniques. While the experience was potent for her life situation at that point in time, the potency of the experience is something she is able to draw on throughout her life.

As practitioners in professional psychology, the challenge is to understand the spiritual dynamic that people experience in their lives. A dualistic approach to the science of psychology contends that psychology, as a science, is based on observable evidence that can be quantified and verified. Spirituality and religious experience have been understood to be outside of this scientific model of psychology. This dualistic approach is inadequate for the practice of psychology today. While psychology is often defined as the science of human behavior, the etymology of the word psychology relays a different focus. The Greek root, *psyche*, refers to *breath, spirit, or soul*, i.e., the animating principle within a person. The animating principle within an individual is the foundation for psychology. Human behavior is nothing more than one of the measurable expressions of that animating principle, just as neuro-electric activity in the brain is another measurable experience of the psyche.

Because psychology is a science, constructs used in psychology must be clearly defined in ways that can be observed and measured. Spirituality continues to be a challenge for the science of psychology precisely because of the difficulty of defining this construct and creating valid and reliable measurements of spirituality within human experience. Recent developments in theory, research, and clinical application provide a more solid basis to operationalize spirituality as a construct in psychology and to observe and measure this construct.

This book draws together theory, research, and application related to the integration of spirituality with the practice of psychology. It is written for students and practitioners to provide a conceptual understanding of the relationship between spirituality and psychology. The text represents a synthesis of and reflection on a variety of sources as well as the author's experience as a clinician, clinical supervisor, graduate level instructor and professional trainer. It will indentify and define the spiritual dimension of human experience. Based on this definition, an integrated model of the self that includes cultural, physiological, cognitive, behavioral, and spiritual dimensions is presented. Case studies will provide an opportunity to explore the application of the integrated model of self. A summary and critique of approaches to spiritual assessment is also included. Finally, ethical issues related to the inclusion of spirituality and mental health are discussed. This book is written to move the conversation about the integration of spirituality within the practice of psychology to greater depth by providing an approach that builds on existing models of mental health practice in the fields of psychology, counseling, and social work.

Chapter 1

Defining Spirituality

The client has been a difficult one for Brenda. When she's met with her supervisor, Brenda often presents this client. The client, an older African American woman with a difficult to manage bipolar disorder, has been Brenda's most challenging client. Brenda wants to do well in this, her first job after completing a master's degree in counseling. She is beginning to think that the client cannot be helped.

In reviewing the case with her supervisor, Brenda reports that she is attempting to use a strength-based approach in working with the client. "When I ask her about how she has solved other problems in life, all she says is 'Jesus got me through.' She does not demonstrate autonomy. If Jesus has to do everything for her, she'll never be responsible for herself."

The supervisor listens to Brenda's frustration. She patiently asks, "Have you considered that autonomy for the client is connected to Jesus. You have decided that "Jesus" represents outside locus of control. Maybe she's talking about "Jesus" inside of her. What do you know about Jesus and your client's life?"

Brenda did not have an answer to the question. The possibility that faith could be an expression of an internal locus of control was something she had not considered. After meeting with her supervisor, Brenda decided to explore this issue with her client.

In the practice of psychology, the definition of constructs is significant. For example, although most people equate the experience of depression as feeling blue, mental health professionals understand the construct "depression" as a mood disorder characterized by a series of particular symptoms. Clinical depression is also the result of changes in the release and uptake of particular neurotransmitters. When a clinician uses the term, "major depressive disorder," psychiatrists, psychologists, counselors, social workers and other mental health professionals all know exactly what is described. The same is true for many other clinical terms like affect, resiliency, or cognitive function.

Spirituality and the Clinician's Experience

When the word "spirituality" is introduced in a clinical setting, mental health professionals are left to define the construct based on their own experience. Subjectivity in the approach to spirituality results from the lack of a standard definition of this construct. Trained to avoid imposing their own thoughts and beliefs onto clients, there is a dissonance created between the clinician's own experience of spirituality and what spirituality could mean in a clinical setting. Even with advanced degrees and years of clinical training, mental health professionals are usually uncertain how to effectively bridge the gap between their own experience and the experience of their clients in regard to spirituality.

At the same time, to understand the role of spirituality in the lives of clients, it is vital that we, as clinicians, understand the experience and scope of spirituality in our own lives. To that end, pause and reflect for a few moments. Recall a time in your life that you would label as spiritual. It doesn't matter whether you think anyone else would use that word for your experience. Consider a particular moment, a specific experience of something spiritual.

Perhaps your experience occurred when walking along a beach or the rim of the Grand Canyon. You experienced yourself differently in relationship to the vast expanse along the horizon. Or your experience may have occurred when you gave birth to a child or were with someone who passed from this life. You may recall a spiritual experience when singing a chorus during a church service or when engaging in a spiritual practice like meditation. It does not matter what the experience was. Instead, recall the experience in all the detail you can. What were you feeling, thinking, experiencing? How has this experience stayed with you?

Having recalled a specific experience in your life, consider this question: what is spirituality? How do you define spirituality?

Spirituality versus Religion

One approach to defining spirituality is by distinguishing it from religion. When this distinction is made, it suggests that spirituality is about some kind of pure experience, or a positive feeling, or something that is a unique aspect of life events. Religion, in turn, is defined in terms of institutional membership, dogma and beliefs, or ritualistic observances. From this distinction, spirituality and religion are understood as unrelated to each other and comprise two separate domains.

While this distinction makes sense from a theoretical perspective, when examining the lives of many people living in the United States today, spirituality and religion cannot be easily confined in separate domains. For some people, spirituality and religion have no connection at all. For other people, spirituality and religion cannot be separated. Perhaps more common is the intertwining of some aspects of religious expression and observance with personal spirituality. At the same time, people often have spiritual experiences apart from their religious practices but may interpret those experiences from the perspective of religious beliefs. In other words, spiritual experience may or may not be related to religious practice, observance, symbols, or beliefs even for a particular individual. Because of this, separating the terms spirituality and religion is no more helpful to a clinician that using them interchangeably.

Spirituality as a Dimension of Human Experience

Spirituality functions in our lives in ways that are both transcendent and imminent. Spirituality is transcendent in that it opens the individual to experience something more than what is tangibly present in a particular situation. Simultaneously, spirituality is imminent in so far as it also draws an individual back to the individual's lived experience. In other words, spirituality functions as a dialectic between intangible concepts and constructs beyond the self, while also providing a heightened sense of integration within the self.

Spirituality is a dimension of human beings, just as our bodies and mental capacities are dimensions of the self. While philosophical, theological and metaphysical writers have expressed this understanding about spirituality for generations, contemporary research in genetics and neurology demonstrate that spirituality is a foundational part of the human makeup.

Genetics and Spirituality

From 1983 to 1990, researchers at the University of Minnesota conducted the landmark study of twins separated at birth and raised by different families. Under the direction of principal investigator, David Lykenn, the study identified a number of common markers between identical and fraternal twins. In general, there was a higher correlation of factors between identical twins than fraternal twins leading to the conclusion of a genetic basis for these commonalities. Among the shared commonalities between twins were similarities in religious values and spiritual feelings. While the correlation was not consistent in terms of religious behavior itself, the study suggested that the correlation of beliefs and feelings toward spirituality may have a genetic basis.

In 2000, Comings, et al., published results of a study using a temperament type indicator and a genotyped at the 48 base pair repeat polymorphism of the DRD4 gene. The results indicated that the DRD4 gene may play a role in what the study defined as spiritual acceptance.

In 2005, Dean Hammer published results of his research on the genetic basis of spirituality in the popular book, *The God Gene: How Faith Is Hardwired Into Our Genes*. While the title is clearly provocative, the research Hammer describes presents evidence that spirituality and self-transcendence has some link to the gene VMAT2. The research suggests a correlation between mystical experience or a sense of the presence of God and this gene.

While the evidence from genetic research is not complete, it does strongly suggest that there is a genetic component of spiritual experience. For our purposes, it does not matter whether such a genetic predisposition to spirituality is an inherent trait in human beings or arose from later cultural adaptation. What is important for the practice of psychology is that genetic research presents a body of evidence supporting an understanding that spirituality is part of the genetic code of human beings. In other words, spirituality is a dimension of who we are as human beings.

Neurology and Spirituality

In his final book, *Island*, British novelist Aldous Huxley writes of a utopian world. Published in 1962, Huxley develops a concept he called *neurotheology*. Sometimes referred to as spiritual neuro-science, the concept suggests that the capacity for religious or spiritual experiences can be found in specific regions of the brain. Over the last decade various magazines have popularized this notion by describing research on a so-called "God spot" in the brain.

While a number of research protocols have been undertaken to determine the existence of a "God spot," a team from the

National Institute of Neurological Disorders and Stroke led by Dr. Jordan Grafman conducted one of the most respected studies. A report on the study, published in March 2009 in *the Proceedings of the National Academy of Sciences* (Kapogiannis, et. al, 2009) and reported on by major media outlets, found that a variety of areas of the brain were activated when study participants were asked about various conceptualizations of God or religious experiences. Based on the findings in this and other similar studies, no clear evidence exists for a particular "God spot" in the brain. Instead, religious and spiritual pursuits involve the various areas of the brain used for thought, analysis, and conjecture.

Extensive research on neurological activity and spiritual practices has demonstrated very positive findings that support the positive benefits of spiritual and religious practice. Neurologist Andrew Newberg and therapist Mark Robert Waldman present major findings in their 2009 book, *How God Changes Your Brain*. The research findings reported demonstrate that a practice of meditation slows the aging of the brain, helps to regulate neurotransmitters, and supports recovery from trauma. Belief in a loving God reduces anxiety, depression, and stress while increasing feelings of security, compassion, and love. Deep prayer and meditation over time permanently change neural pathways resulting in a more positive perception of reality.

While Newberg and Waldman are part of the Center for Spirituality and the Mind at the University of Pennsylvania, several other major research universities in the United States also investigate the interconnections between spirituality and the brain. Consistent in all of the research is that belief and spiritual practice impact the brain as well as physical and mental health. Chapter six presents additional research on the relationship between spirituality and mental health. For the purpose of defining spirituality for use in mental health, neurological research supports the understanding that spirituality and spiritual experience are rooted in the brain.

Operationally Defining Spirituality

The human genetic code and human neurology provide a foundation for understanding spirituality as a dimension of human experience. As a dimension of human experience, spirituality has the unique function of drawing human beings beyond self i.e., self-transcendence, while also allowing for an integration of transcendent dimensions of experience within ordinary experience.

Spirituality may then be defined as *the dimension of human experience that enables an individual to create, encounter or discover meaning, purpose, and value in life.*

Spiritual experiences can result in a number of different ways. They can be created by using rituals or specific practices, encountered in life events like the birth of a child or being with a loved one who dies, or discovered while hiking in the woods. It is the nature of these experiences to draw the individual beyond self toward the recognition of subjective transcendent meaning, purpose, or value. The transcendent meaning, purpose or value becomes integrated with the self, resulting in the individual coming to a subjective awareness of her or his own life having meaning, purpose, or value. There is a dialectic cycle in terms of the role spirituality plays in an individual's life. For example, the fact that engaging in a particular meditation practice is purposeful, the individual's life derives a greater sense of purpose. For another person because hiking in the woods one day led to the realization that the person should make a particular change in life was meaningful, the person's life takes on a particular sense of meaning. Or someone who marries a soul mate experiences married life with that individual as valuable. Spirituality is that dimension of human experience that enables the individual to create, discover, or encounter meaning, purpose, and value. Because of the meaning, purpose, and value associated with the experience, a person understands life as meaningful, purposeful, and valuable.

The Integration of Spirituality

Returning to the earlier exercise presented at the beginning of this chapter, consider again your own experience of spirituality. In what way did you create, discover or encounter the experience? Has the experience taken on a particular meaning, purpose or value in your life? In what way has that experience made your life more meaningful, purposeful, or valuable?

By considering spirituality from a strength-based phenomenological perspective, clinicians are better able to identify the role of spirituality within a client's life to support a therapeutic process toward greater integration no matter what religious beliefs or spiritual practices a client uses as a reference. From this perspective, spirituality as a dimension of self is an integral aspect of personal growth and transformation.

While spirituality is a dimension of the self, it is just one dimension of the self that is integrated with other dimensions. The challenge for psychology is to understand how this dimension of the self promotes healthy functioning in an individual's life.

As Brenda met with her client in their next session, she once again asked the client how she made it through difficult times in the past. The client responded, "Honey, I keep telling you: Jesus always gets me through." Brenda asked, "Can you tell me more about what that means?" The client responded, "If you knew him, you'd understand. He's in me. He's all around me. I don't go anywhere without him. When I'm troubled, I close my eyes and talk to him. Sometimes I wait, but I always hear him inside of me." Brenda began to understand that the client had internal dialogues with Jesus. She continued, "What difference does talking to Jesus inside of you make when times are difficult?" With a few simple questions, Brenda could understand more about how the client's spirituality was a vital internal resource.

Chapter 2

The Model of the Integrated Self

The team gathered in a conference room. The unit's nurse manager chaired the meeting. The social worker, chaplain, dietician, and home care coordinator would be present for the entire meeting. Intermittently, physicians and a psychologist would also attend. This was the nursing unit's weekly team meeting designed to increase the level of integrated care for patients.

When a particular physician and psychologist arrived, the topic quickly moved to Mrs. Garcia who was recovering from hip replacement surgery. Although the surgery was successful, Mrs. Garcia was slow to recover. The psychologist's evaluation resulted in a diagnosis of major depressive disorder. Mrs. Garcia was lethargic, displayed a flat affect, and showed no interest in food.

Each member of the team reported observations about Mrs. Garcia's condition. While they all understood each other, it was as though each team member spoke a different language.

In her initial report, the chaplain presented Mrs. Garcia's religious affiliation, frequency of church attendance, and reported that no particular beliefs or practices were in conflict with the medical care received. After there was some further discussion among the team members, the chaplain sighed and said, "She doesn't have anything to live for. There's no motivation for her to get better."

The social worker followed suit, "I didn't want to put it that way, but I think it's true. Her husband died a miserable death from cancer after working as a migrant farmer for years. She's been living with her daughter who hasn't had stable relation-

ships with men. The daughter's current boyfriend appears to be an abusive alcoholic. That daughter's oldest son was recently killed in a gang shooting."

The practice of psychology focuses on the treatment of mental disorders in order to increase an individual's level of functioning. As a Western science, psychology measures human functioning based on observable behavior. In other words, mental health is understood as different from physical health or social status.

Over the last two decades, there has been an increased awareness in the practice of psychology of other dimensions of human experience as they relate to an individual's mental health. For instance, mental health practitioners have become more aware of the neurological basis of many mental disorders. State licensing boards require at least some expertise in cultural competency for mental health practitioners. Models of treatment have also been critiqued from a wide variety of perspectives including women, sexual minorities, and various racial and ethnic groups because of the limitations of both the theoretical basis of psychology and behaviorally based definitions of healthy functioning. While these things have broadened awareness to the limitations of the current practice of psychology as well as a dualistic approach that focuses on one dimension of an individual to the exclusion of others, the application of psychology has not been able to adopt holistic or integrationist approaches.

Mental health clinicians need a more integrated approach for treatment to address spirituality and other aspects of human experience so that psychology can support the growth and integration of the whole person. Some clinicians use vague models based on concepts like the integration of body, mind, and spirit. Other clinicians draw Jungian typologies and archetypes. There are also clinicians who draw on approaches to under-standing humanity from various cultures or world religions.

Applying a therapeutic model that conveys the complexity of human experience while also maintaining the integrity of the science of psychology is a challenge to the practice of psychology at the beginning of the twenty-first century. Models in the practice of psychology tend to focus on a particular set of assumptions related to human experience to the exclusion of other dimensions. This has led many clinicians to adopt an eclectic approach to therapy. Approaching clinical work from a more unified and integrated model has the potential result for offering more effective therapeutic practice and more significant clinical outcomes. To this end, the work of Dutch psychologist, Adrian van Kaam, offers particular insights.

Van Kaam began work in psychology at Duquesne University as founder of a specialized department in phenomenological psychology. He later established the Institute of Formative Spirituality, a graduate program also at Duquesne University. Following in the tradition of European philosophers and existential psychologists, van Kaam sought to articulate what he called the science of human formation. Much like the work of developmental psychologist Urie Bronfenbrenner, van Kaam understood human development to evolve over the lifespan. This evolution is multidimensional and holistic.

While van Kaam published extensively, his writing is not commonly known because of his decision to employ language that is outside of the mainstream of psychology. Further, while his work is a synthesis of the research of others, van Kaam resisted attribution to the original thinkers who were founda-tional to his endeavors. The strength of his writing remains the synthesis of a great deal of theory and research in psychology along with an understanding of the great traditions of world religion. This strength is quickly lost because of his obtuse use of language to describe his integrated model.

As a clinician, I have adapted key aspects van Kaam's work, attempting to better reflect the original sources that are the foundation for his writing. This adaptation is a reduction of van Kaam's original work. The model proposed here is an attempt to convey commonly understood constructs in contemporary psychology related to other key theorists.

The Model of the Integrated Self

In this integrated model, the individual holds within self four basic dimensions. Each dimension is a constituent part of the self or ego. To fail to consider any one of the four dimensions is to disregard the scope of human experience and the integral way each dimension is part of an individual's identity. Experience in one dimension is intertwined with the other dimensions. Those dimensions are the sociohistorical, the embodied, the engaging, and the spiritual.

These dimensions should be understood as constituent aspects of the self or ego. The self is comprised of each of these dimensions. An analogy for these dimensions can be found in physics. The world as we know and experience it is comprised of three dimensions: length, width, and height. While theoretical physicists can postulate a universe with fewer dimensions or more dimensions, such a universe is outside of the experience of the world in which we live. In a similar way, the self is comprised of four dimensions: the sociohistorical, the embodied, the engaging, and the spiritual. To take any of these dimensions away is to diminish the self and reduce human experience into something unrecognizable. All four dimensions are engaged in any human activity, even though a particular activity may primarily reflect or impact on particular dimension.

The Sociohistorical Dimension

Born at the turn of the twentieth century, Russian psychologist Lev Vygotsky articulated a structuralist understanding of childhood development. As a child biologically develops, cognitive development also occurs based on knowledge mediated to the child by the surrounding culture. The child then internalizes knowledge provided by the culture. This process of internalizing culturally-based information leads to the development of cognition and speech.

From the child's earliest development, parents and other caretakers interact with a child based on patterns that reflect the culture into which the child was born. This interaction mediates information about how to organize one's life, social roles, and how to interpret experience. The development of neural pathways is related to this interaction. Vygotsky understood that this mediation conveys to the child patterns for organizing thoughts and the interpretation of experience. These patterns for organizing thoughts give rise to speech. Vygotsky described language acquisition as a process based on the development of cognition that was articulated in speech. In other words, a child knows to call out "Mama!" because that information was mediated from the culture through the parents and caregivers to the child that identity the female birth-giver as mother. This mediation conveys to the child information about all aspects of life: social roles, relationships, values as well as intangible concepts like hopes and dreams for the future. Throughout childhood, culture continues to meditate lessons about one's own identity and sense of self, gender roles, social behavior, and ambitions to strive for.

Vygotsky's structuralist theory of cognitive development postulates that culture is a foundational aspect for the development of the self or ego. Vygotsky's understanding of culture as part of individual identity is fundamentally different from what is commonly understood in much literature about cultural competence. From a cultural competence perspective, culture is conceived as something an individual has or is part of, as though culture is outside of the self, like a social support network or particular interests for leisure. Vygotsky understood culture as mediated through childhood development and internalized during growth and cognitive development. Further, culture is not static but dynamic. Just as culture is a foundation for the cognitive development and evolution of the self, so too the individual's participation in a culture leads to the evolution of culture.

Culture, in this sense, is not about customs, celebrations, and cuisine. Instead, culture is fundamentally a way of thinking about and organizing life and all that it contains. An individual's way of thinking, which is manifested in speech and behavior, is rooted in the individual's culture. Culture is mediated through the social context of care-giving in early childhood and continues through the child's growth toward adulthood.

A simple example of the role culture plays within an individual is the acceptable amount of space between two speakers. In some cultures, speakers are close to each other, perhaps touching or standing intentionally close enough to smell each other's breath or body odor. In other cultures, distance in maintained and physical touch is considered impolite. These culturally-based behaviors are mediated to a child in early development and become part of the individual. Later in life, this behavior is simply part of how the individual behaves and communicates. The individual may learn that when speaking to people from other cultures, the distance between speakers should be adjusted to accommodate the cultural differences. In the end, there is a certain distance between speakers that pre-reflectively seems right to the individual.

Based on the sociohistorical dimension, an individual develops an internal understanding about the individual's own identity in relationship to others; appropriate goals and ambitions in life; appropriate patterns for relationships; the value of persons, places and things; customs; and ways to understand and interact with the broader world. The sociohistorical dimension internalizes aspects of the individual's culture so that how one views self, others, and the world is, in a sense, set as default programming. For example, a person who was born and grew up in a collectivist culture where the needs of the family or community come before the needs of the individual may move to the United States and learn about what it means to live in an individualistic culture where the needs of the individual come before the needs of others. Yet the person has first internalized the relationship patterns of the collectivist culture and only steps out of them with deliberate effort. For Vygotsky, this is because the culture is part of the individual and the individual is part of the culture. In other words, the sociohistorical dimension described by Vygotsky is a primary aspect of the integrated self.

The Embodied Dimension

Human beings are embodied creatures. From within our bodies, we experience the world around us and people experience us. Our thoughts, actions, aspirations, and affections are experienced in and through our bodies.

An unfortunate aspect of English is that it causes us to speak our embodiment in an inaccurate way. In English, we state that we have a body. We refer to it, as I just did, as "our body."

However, the body is not a possession. Instead, we are our bodies and our bodies are us.

Consider for a moment this illustration. Imagine awakening one morning with the flu and a fever. It's nothing serious but something that will pass in a day or two. Reflect on that experience. Picture it. You're lying in bed, a place most of us look forward to being at the end of each day. Our beds are warm, comforting places to relax and rest. Yet on this morning with a flu and fever, you move your hand from where the sheets are warm to where they are cold and you shiver. You pull your arm back to the warm place as quickly as possible. The bed has become unfriendly.

You get out of bed to make your way to the bathroom. This short trip, which you can typically make half-asleep in the dark without any real effort, on this morning with the flu and a fever becomes a surreal experience. It is unclear if you are spinning, or the room is spinning, or if someone moved the bathroom from its usual place. You may have to grasp onto furniture to steady yourself or orient yourself in the direction you want to go.

The aroma of freshly brewed coffee fills the house as a coffee maker drips a fresh brew. Fresh coffee! What a pleasant aroma! Except on this morning with the flu, the smell makes you a bit nauseated.

On this morning, a tiny virus is working its way through your body. While the virus does not represent a major change in your body, the experience of self and the world around you has changed. It isn't just that your body is ill. Instead, you are ill and experiencing a pronounced sense of disease. This is an experience of embodiment.

Over the course of our lives, our bodies change, grow, and in time, diminish. As physical changes occur, how we experience ourselves and the ways others experience us also changes, grows, and evolves.

In adolescence, youths experience a pronounced period of

physical growth. In a few months time, things that they looked up to become things they look down on. Things that used to be far away become items at their fingertips. It's not just that their bodies have changed, but that their experience of themselves and the world around them has changed.

Similarly, as people grow older, the body doesn't respond to things as quickly and easily as it did in our youth. Perhaps the change in response begins with increased stiffness or a creaking of bones. In time, it may seem as though our bodies betray us when doing favorite activities become very challenging. These physical changes bring a diminishment of our sense of self as well as different relationships to those around us.

The embodied dimension includes our physical and physiological development and all the changes that occur naturally over time as well as unexpected changes related to illness, disease, or traumatic events. In the practice of psychology, it is understood that emotions are rooted in this embodied dimension as part of the neuro-chemicals that form the roots of emotions. Mental disorders also have an embodied dimension because of their neurological foundations. While there is an acknowledgement in psychology of the physical and neurological basis for mental disorders and an individual's capacity to function on the psychological level, issues related to the body are left to other specialists in the field of medicine. Yet everything an individual experiences in life is experienced in and through the body. Conversely, bodily experiences significantly impact an individual's ability to function in a healthy way on a psychological level. In a fundamental way, the embodied dimension of self is a constituent part to all of our experiences.

The Engaging Dimension

The engaging dimension is the part of self that engages with the world through relationships, works, hobbies, activities, interests and the multiple ways we participate in life. The engaging dimension holds particular significance in psychology and is the dimension most associated with personal identity and the self.

The engaging dimension often becomes the primary way to understand identity. For example, in Western culture, people are often defined by their occupation. The first question asked when meeting a new person is, "What do you do?" The connection between personal identity and occupation can be seen across lifespan development. Children and adolescents are oriented toward becoming something. "What do you want to be when you grow up?" is a question frequently asked of a child. When youth struggle with the question, a typical response is often, "You have time. You'll figure it out" which while giving permission to make a choice over time, underscores the importance of this life-choice in regard to identity. In adulthood and later adulthood, job loss and retirement are often experiences of the loss of identity because one no longer engages in the activity that has defined self. This loss is also felt by parents whose children grow and leave home. The loss of engaging as parents can be a loss of the sense of self.

Another aspect of the engaging dimension as a source of identity is family relationship. In collectivist cultures, family relationship is the prime component for personal identity. The family or clan takes precedence over individual personality, behavior, or desires. In Western culture, being married or in a long-term coupled relationship creates identity as do relationships between parents and children. Loss of these relationships through divorce or the children leaving home when reaching adulthood may also impact an individual's sense of identity.

The engaging dimension focuses on all the things an individual does and the way the individual functions. This dimension is the realm of the practice of psychology. In mental health, behavioral symptoms are assessed and levels of functioning are measured. These external attributes of engagement in the world are used as windows into the inner world of mental health. To restore functioning by alleviating behavioral symptoms or by making interventions to improve specific skills in functioning is understood as the goal of mental health therapy.

Psychologists, social workers, counselors, marriage and family therapists, and mental health professionals working in schools, hospitals and community centers primarily focus their work on the engaging dimension of the self. This is our area of specialization. The integrated model of the self does not suggest that professionals in the practice of psychology abandon this specialization in an attempt to become specialists in all of the dimensions of self. Instead, greater appreciation for the multiple dimensions of the self can lead to greater understanding of the role of those working in professions related to psychology. While the engaging dimension of the self is of great importance, under-standing it as one aspect of the integrated self will lead to greater balance for an individual.

The Spiritual Dimension

In addition to the sociohistorical, embodied, and engaging dimensions of human experience, there is also the spiritual dimension. The previous chapter explained that the spiritual dimension is part of who we are as human beings on a genetic and neurological level. At the same time, spirituality cannot be reduced to genetics or neurology. It is a dimension of self that is unique, as are the other three dimensions.

While those who study theology, metaphysics, or spiritualism address an understanding of spirituality as a realm outside of the individual, within the mental health professions, it is vital for us to consider spirituality as a dimension of the integrated self in much the same way as culture has been understood as a dimension of self.

The spiritual dimension of the integrated self is that dimension that allows and enables us to experience something more than what is already given in the other dimensions. The spiritual dimension is that aspect of who we are that adds value to human experience from the other dimensions.

The spiritual dimension is a dimension of transcendence toward something more than is apparent in the experiences of the other dimensions. It is a dimension of aspiring to find or discover something greater than is part of the other dimensions. It is also transcendence in and through the other dimensions. In other words, this "more than" spiritual dimension is experienced as part of the other dimensions. It is a transcendence that is within real life.

The spiritual dimension is evident within the engaging dimension when work is transformed from routine and drudgery to something meaningful; when the day-to-day sacrifices of a long-term relationship and family life are experienced as something of value; or when the tedium of hobbies like gardening or needle-point are experienced as valuable and enjoyable.

The spiritual dimension is manifested through the embodied dimension when the experience of touching another becomes an act of love or care; when pain, as in childbirth, is a source of joy; when physical exhaustion from dancing at someone's wedding or from exercise and body building become purposeful because there is something more than just exhaustion taking place.

The spiritual dimension is often rooted in the sociohistorical dimension as aspects of one's culture form the sources for meaning, purpose, and value in an individual's life. Cultural customs, foods, and icons take on particular value as national anthems, the raising of a flag, singing a Christmas carol, or gathering for a holiday meal become something more than songs or routine habits. Perhaps even more deeply rooted are cultural values that shape an individual's life in potent ways including a culture's understanding of the role of parenthood, success, or specific belief systems.

The spiritual dimension of the integrated self may be expressed in religious idioms but is not limited to religious language. For example, consider an individual who goes for a walk in the woods to sort out thoughts about a particularly stressful experience at work. On this walk, the person pauses and watches and listens to a bird perched in a tree who is chirping in a pleasant manner. A person who practices a certain set of religious beliefs may interpret the experience as God sending the song-bird with a message about the need to take more time to relax rather than focus on work stress. Another person may describe the same experience by stating that by watching the bird, there was an inspiration about the need to relax rather than focus on work stress. The presence or lack of religious idiom is not what constitutes the spiritual dimension. Instead, it is the dynamic through which an ordinary life event, hearing a bird sing, is understood as more than just a chirping bird. The transcendent dimension of the spiritual dimension results in the discovery of something meaningful about the bird's song, which in turn adds meaning and value to the person's life.

The spiritual dimension of the self is operative in and through the other dimensions, opening those dimensions to something "more than," infusing them with meaning, or purpose, or value.

Integration: the Four Dimensions as One

For the purpose of analysis, the four dimensions of self have been described in somewhat separate terms. Yet the experience of self is fundamentally unified and integrated. When experiencing self and the world around us, each dimension is present even though one aspect may be more pronounced than another.

For example, each morning I spend time engaged in a meditation practice. Coming from a family and culture that valued prayer and religious observance, my meditation practice has particular sociohistorical roots, even if it doesn't take the same form of prayer I remember from my parents and grandparents. These sociohistorical roots do convey certain values for and beliefs about the practice. On the embodied dimension, I sit in a particular position, I breathe, and I relax. Over 20 to 30 minutes, my respiration changes. I also understand that there are particular changes in neurological activity because of this practice. There is also specific engagement in this practice of meditation. I begin by reading a portion of a sacred text, I close my eyes, and I turn my attention inward. There are things that I do in this practice that form a routine. My experience of this meditation practice is something more than what occurs on the sociohistorical, embodied, and engaging dimension. I have a particular set of beliefs about what is occurring during the time in meditation that is much "more than" just sitting in a chair. This "more than" spiritual experience transcends sitting silently in a chair for a period of time to a time that is meaningful to me and in turn, provides a certain sense of meaning in my life. I am purposeful about how I engage in this time of sitting silently in a chair that in turn infuses a certain purpose in my life. I value the time of silence, which also adds to my experience of life as valuable.

This same dynamic is operative when considering specifically religious or spiritual endeavors or when examining other aspects of life including work, maintaining relationships, moving through the process of aging or loss, or choosing a career. The spiritual dimension of self enables us to create, discover or encounter meaning, purpose or value in and through the socio-historical, embodied, and engaging dimensions of self. Meaning, purpose, and value may be understood by the individual through specific religious metaphors ("God called me to do this with my life") or in descriptions without religious or spiritual references ("I find my work fulfilling.")

Mental Health Practice and the Four Dimensions of Self

Mental health practitioners assess behavioral functioning in regard to the sense of self, relationships, work, and various social environments. The theoretical models employed in the practice of psychology primarily focus on the engaging dimension of the self.

Over the last twenty years, there has been increased awareness in mental health professions about the embodied and sociohistorical dimensions. This has led toward a more integrative therapeutic approach than what was often found in past generations of psychological practice. However, the primary work in psychology remains the focus on the engaging dimension of self. The goal of therapy is to improve an individual's functioning in the world.

The integrated model presented is not meant to replace a clinician's existing theoretical orientation or therapeutic practice. Instead, the intention is to broaden the view of therapeutic work. Physicians and psychiatrists continue to specialize in matters related to the embodied self. Sociologists and cultural anthropologists offer specialized insights into the sociohistorical dimension of self. The spectrum of mental health professionals, psychologists, counselors, social workers, marriage and family therapists, case managers, etc., provide particular expertise regarding the engaging dimension of self. No matter the primary perspective of the specialist (a counselor, a physician, or sociologist), the person remains an integrated individual because identity is comprised of all four dimensions. In other words, when a structural family therapist reframes a family system problem, the result is better functioning in the family as well as a family member experiencing less physical stress, becoming more productive at work, and generally feeling more hopeful for the future.

Traditional health and mental health training maintains a focus on a specific dimension but an intervention on any dimension impacts all of the other dimensions. This includes the spiritual dimension.

In Western culture, the professionals associated with the spiritual dimension of life have been clergy. As Western culture has changed in the post-modern era, clergy may not be the ones viewed by individuals as possessing expertise for the role of spiritual teacher. Further, in a multicultural society, there are few common metaphors to describe spiritual experience. Many people in the United States today draw on metaphors and experience from the religious background of the family, practices like yoga and relaxation, and from reading a variety of literature that incorporates themes of spirituality including business leadership, sports performance, or motivational training.

Clients come to mental health professionals with the hope of addressing problems related to their life engagements and functioning, but also present themes related to the spiritual dimension of life as manifested in the engaging dimension.

Appropriate mental health treatment does not call for abandoning proven models and interventions used in the practice of psychology. Instead, the integrated model of self invites clinicians to consider how the treatment of mental health issues is related to the systemic that makes up the self.

After a long silence, the chaplain commented, "She is very involved in her church. I thought they had a very active pastoral support program. Has anyone visited from the church?" The nurse manager reported that Mrs. Garcia didn't want the church notified that she was in the hospital.

The psychologist noted, "She doesn't seem to want to talk to me. Maybe the chaplain can have more success in changing how she thinks about her situation. Cognitive therapy is often helpful for people like her."

The physician agreed, "There's nothing wrong with her physically that can't be addressed with regular physical therapy. There are no surgical complications. She's strong and healthy enough for therapy."

Hearing what was said, the nurse manager began to formulate a treatment plan for Mrs. Garcia. The chaplain would work with Mrs. Garcia to identify cognitive patterns inferring with her recovery. The chaplain would also obtain Mrs. Garcia's permission to notify her church. Once the church was notified, the social worker would work with the church visitors to assess additional support resources in Mrs. Garcia's community. The chaplain added, "While social support from her church will be helpful, we need to identify how she's gotten through difficult times in the past. We also need to know is there's anything in her life that has meaning or that gives her a sense of purpose. I'll see her later today. Whatever I find will be in the chart so that everyone else can build on it."

Chapter 3

Mental Health as Living from the Integrated Self

Jerome was someone who never imagined he'd see a counselor. A strong and confident man, Jerome saw himself as having a handle on things. That was up until about a year ago.

After high school, Jerome worked a few different jobs until finally getting a good position at the plant. After twenty years at the plant, making a pretty good salary with benefits, the plant closed. The company was transferring operations to another country.

Jerome's wife has been working full time. With his unemployment benefits, the family, which includes two teenage children, has been able to keep their lives together. But Jerome doesn't know what to do for the future. The jobs available in town pay a fraction of what he was making and just a bit more than unemployment benefits. He only has a high school education. His children are looking forward to college in a few years. Although they are better off than some of his friends who have lost homes and live off credit cards, Jerome knows that he needs to find a direction for himself and his family.

When he was hanging out at the barber shop, he read an article in a newspaper about men who lost their jobs starting small businesses. He mentioned it to the guys at the barber shop. They told him that he made the best barbeque in town. He could open a barbeque take-out place. It seemed like an interesting idea. He liked to cook. For years, at church dinners, he always made the barbeque and people could never get enough. Some folks had offered to pay him for it, but he never took it seriously. He wondered if this was the time to do something he enjoyed.

With free career counseling available through the outplacement services from work, Jerome made an appointment to see a counselor. He thought that a counselor may be able to help him make this kind of decision.

The integrated model of the self suggests that the fundamental goal of the therapeutic process is the further integration of the four dimensions of an individual: the sociohistorical, the embodied, the engaging, and the spiritual. Integration results in a more balanced and fulfilled way of living. Underlying this broad therapeutic goal is the belief that the process of evolution to greater integration of the four dimensions of self is the fundamental process of human development. Therapeutic intervention is a tool to help support this natural developmental process. To that end, balanced integration of self enables one to live in a fully and healthy life from a holistic perspective.

How can clinicians working in therapeutic environments measure the process of a client's integration? What constitutes progress toward an increased level of balance in living? Is this balance different from one person than another? These questions are fundamental to understanding both the therapeutic process and the larger process of personal integration.

Congruence

In the 1960s, Carl Rogers explored the actualizing tendency of people to grow into what he called the true self. At the heart of this growth or evolution was the concept of congruence. Congruence is a kind of harmony among the dimensions of the self. While the dimensions of the self cannot be separated from each other but coexist as dynamic whole, congruence moves toward a fundamental integration among the dimensions of the self. To be incongruent is not just pretending to be someone different from oneself. Incongruence is living out of an illusory sense of self. In contrast, congruence is a relaxed stability rooted in self-knowledge and equilibrium among the various dimensions of the self.

While congruence is a humanistic concept, in the common practice of therapy today, it is usually understood through the lens of cognitive-behavioral therapeutic goals. Clinicians' view of congruence is based on a client achieving goals that the client sets at the beginning of therapeutic process. When the goals are met, it is understood that the client has become more congruent with self, is more integrated, and psychologically healthier. While cognitive-behavioral goals provide insight into some aspects of the engaging dimension of self, as has been discussed, the individual is more than what is reflected through the engaging dimension of self as measured by cognitive-behavioral goals.

Rogers' own description of congruence is more expansive than goal oriented therapeutic evaluation suggests. However, Rogers did not take into account the sociohistorical, embodied, and spiritual dimensions to self that are part of the integrated model. Because of that, a more expensive approach to congruence is needed than Rogers' humanistic approach.

Existential Congruence

While Rogers used the term congruent to describe a person whose inner self corresponded to the person's outer behavior and affect, a broader understanding of congruence is needed to reflect an understanding of the multidimensional integrated self. *Existential congruence* encompasses the cognitive-behavioral approach but goes further to include the broader domain of the individual's consciousness of inner experience as it relates to the way an individual understands self from a holistic perspective. Existential congruence considers four aspects: an understanding of one's deepest self, personal abilities, external limitations, and active compassion for self and others.

Understanding of One's Deepest Self

Existential congruence assesses whether behavior is congruent with consciousness of self. The conscious understanding of self includes cognition, thoughts and emotions as well as all the various aspects of the individual's understanding of self. That may include familial or social roles, goals and ambitions, cultural identity or any of the identities of self that emerge from the various dimensions of self. It also includes the ways in which the individual finds life meaningful and valuable. The conscious understanding of self is the lived experience gathered over the lifespan.

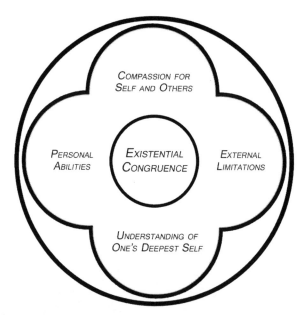

An existential approach to congruence explores the degree to which the individual understands the life currently led or changes made in life to be representative of the individual's understanding of the deepest sense of self. In other words, to what degree does an individual believe that he or she is living out inner potential and socio-cultural expectations for self? This aspect of congruence is often related to aspects of mental health like career counseling, but it is more than an occupational concern. It also involves the individual's understanding of self in regard to relationships, roles in family or community, or other personal endeavors like hobbies and interests. For example, while a person may find a certain degree of satisfaction in a chosen job or career, that career may not meet a heartfelt desire to care for others the way engaging in volunteer or charitable work on weekends offers the person. Existential consonance considers how the broader dimensions of self and the fundamental desires to manifest self in the world are operative in a person's life.

Personal Abilities

In addition to fulfilling an individual's potential about what to do or to be in life, a person's abilities play a significant role. The desire or dream to achieve particular goals or a particular method of self-expression is not the same as having the ability to do so. An existential approach to congruence considers the balance between the inner sense of self to engage in activities along with the person's abilities. For example, a person may have a great passion for classical music. However, the person's ability to play a musical instrument may be limited for a variety of reasons. While the person may visualize self as a great pianist, the lack of ability prevents this from occurring. If such a person has an ability to write, perhaps the passion for music and the ability to write could result in the individual becoming a noteworthy reviewer or critic of classical music.

There is a level of dissonance many people experience in life between the desire to do or become something while not having the ability to manifest the achievement. An aspect of congruence from an existential perspective is to live within the limitations a person has. Many of those limitations are based on a person's characteristics and genetic abilities. These are unlikely to change. Instead, learning to appreciate and affirm those limitations is related to an individual's ability to affirm self for who one is rather than struggling to be who one is not.

External Limitations

Some limitations are external to us. Existential congruence also considers these external limitations. Factors such as economic conditions, personal responsibilities, access to resources and many other issues can limit a person's ability to engage in life differently to follow particular dreams. For example, parents frequently make sacrifices of self to provide for children. These sacrifices are often based on external limitations that cause the parents to make choices often putting the needs of the children first. Or people in one part of the world have different opportunities available to them from those in others parts of the world, often regardless of ability. When faced with external limitations, the task becomes sorting out when it is appropriate to live within the limitations of life and when to push beyond them. For example, there would not have been a Civil Rights movement in the United States if some individuals did not believe that being true to self meant to push out of the external limitations placed by racism. Pushing beyond external limitations is often the dynamic at work in the case of heroic action. However, it may also be an appropriate choice for others to live within external limitations in order to address other responsibilities, which could include ensuring family stability or developing some other aspect of one's life.

Typically, in a cognitive-behavioral or behavioral approach to the understanding of therapeutically goals, the focus is accepting external limitations as generally appropriate and helping an individual to work toward functioning within acceptable social norms. An existential approach more carefully attempts to discern when it is healthy for an individual to function outside of society's norms and when is it not.

Compassion for Self and Others

Ultimately, over the life course, an individual has to reconcile the understanding of who that she or he understands self to be and how life should be lived. Such decisions are made within the context and realities of limited abilities and external limits that are part of everyone's life. Resolution of this tension as part of congruence requires living with compassion toward self. Living with compassion begins by affirming self with the dreams, hopes, and potentials one has. It also is demonstration of compassion for self as a limited being. Compassion toward self is built on the maintenance of basic self-esteem. Self-esteem is affirming oneself for who one is. Self-esteem is an acceptance of self as having both certain abilities and particular limitations. Compassion goes further by not just accepting self as an individual with abilities and limitations but also caring for self in a way that acknowledges that loss of a dream and desires for life to be different. For example, a writer can affirm the level of ability he or she has for the craft of writing. That's a demonstration of self-esteem. Compassion for self recognizes that there was also a dream to be a bestselling author, but that one probably cannot write at that level. Compassion understands the dream, the loss of the dream and the movement toward acceptance of being who one authentically is as a writer with particular abilities and limitations.

As compassion for self grows, an individual is also better able to experience compassion for others who struggle with movement toward greater congruence. The development of compassion for self and others recognizes that other people live with a tension in resolving the tension between a sense of self with particular potential but also with limitations.

Recognizing that Jerome was awkward in meeting with a mental health professional, the career counselor talked conversationally to Jerome to build rapport while trying to understand his situation. After some time, she said, "I'd like to make some suggestions about how I can be helpful to you. I know that you want to get the most of this time with me as possible." Jerome agreed. She continued, "There are two ways I can be of help. One is to provide you with information and resources on how to start a small business. You are right. Across the country, many men in your situation are doing that. It can be a great thing to do but there are also risks The second thing I can do is to be a sounding board and ask some questions to help you make the decision about whether this is the right direction for you."

Jerome paused for a moment and said, "I need both things. But right now, I really need help with the decision. Just because people think I can do this doesn't mean I should open a restaurant." The counselor agreed. "I can give you some material to read on small business start-ups to take home today. You can look at them for next time. But with the rest of our time today, let's start looking at a few aspects of this decision. This is just the beginning of our discussion on these topics, but we should consider if the decision is right for you, how it will impact you and your family, what resources and abilities you have to support this decision, and what limitations you will face." Jerome became very serious. "Talking about these things makes a whole lot of sense. There's a lot to consider in making the right decision."

Chapter 4

Therapeutic Application Based on the Model of the Integrated Self

The integrated model of self enables a mental health professional an approach to the complex experience of an individual. It provides a way to understand how spirituality functions within the experience of the individual and underscores that psychological experience is intertwined with the other complex dimensions of the self.

To better understand both the model and how it is helpful in the practice of psychology, two case studies are examined and discussed based on this model. The cases presented here are clients with whom I previously worked. Their names and identifying information have been changed to safe-guard their anonymity.

The Case of Karen

Karen was a 33-year-old Native American woman. She was diagnosed with Chronic Fatigue Immune Deficiency Syndrome (CFIDS) as a result of a chemical exposure. Because of the CFIDS, Karen gave up her apartment and living on her own and moved in with her mother. Her mother had been living alone.

Prior to this diagnosis, Karen was very active. She completed eight years of service in the military with an honorable discharge. She was very proud of her military service. Following discharge, Karen enrolled in a local community college and went on to complete her bachelors at a state university. Until the CFIDS, she maintained a 3.8 GPA. Her final semester, with the diagnosis of CFIDS, resulted with a 2.1 GPA.

In our first session, Karen stated that she was lethargic, in bed most of the day, and found basic activities of daily life to be exhausting. She stated that if she did not recover, she had nothing to live for. There is no indication that she would harm herself at that time. Karen repeatedly stated that she had nothing to live for. She explained that in her culture, someone like her would have been left to sit on an ice floe and die with dignity. She went on to explain that the only thing she wanted to do was to be useful. She insisted that relationships were of no interest to her. She says that she did not make attachments to people and that the only times she had been happy in life was when she was useful. She had no energy for any activities and her physical prognosis was not clear.

Case Analysis Based on the Integrated Model of Self
Karen has come to therapy because of problems she is experiencing in her life following a diagnosis with Chronic Fatigue Immune Deficiency Syndrome. This medical issue, primarily rooted in the embodied dimension of the self, impacted Karen on the engaging, sociohistorical, and spiritual dimensions of self.

The Embodied Dimension
Because of the chemical exposure in her apartment, Karen was physically ill. Like all illnesses, Chronic Fatigue Immune Deficiency Syndrome (CFIDS) impacts all dimensions of the self. Chronic illnesses, like CFIDS, present sufferers with particular challenges because the Syndrome manifests a wide variety of symptoms that are not easily treated. The disease can cycle or remain constant for years at a time. Treatment can vary a great deal from one person with this Syndrome to another.

The Engaging Dimension
Working in the practice of psychology as a therapist, counselor, or social worker, one would typically begin by identifying Karen's experience from the perspective of her engagements. Her

life radically changed. Karen went from being an active, independent young woman who demonstrated a certain level of competency to moving in with her mother for care. This change is contrary to the expected developmental order for a single woman in her early thirties. In addition, she could not function in ways to which she had grown accustomed.

Because the changes in the engaging dimension are the result of something that occurred on the embodied dimension due to her physical illness, obtaining a clear history becomes very important. From the history, I learned that Karen was the youngest of three children. Her father had a long history of alcohol addiction and left the family when she was in grade school. While she is aware that her father lives in another part of the country, none of the siblings have any regular contact with him. All three siblings left home upon turning 18 years old. Karen opted to join the United States Air Force. When she enlisted, she was told that she would be trained in linguistics, which was an important interest of hers. Her dream was to do work in the preservation of Native American languages. Joining the Air Force was both a way to leave home and to move toward the fulfillment of a meaningful dream to be useful to Native People.

Her cultural tribal affiliation was with a Northern Canadian subarctic nation. It was her grandfather's generation that relocated to the United States in pursuit of employment. She was raised in a major metropolitan area and had little direct contact with her tribe. She had never visited the tribal lands but as an adult she learned to speak the language of her people.

Karen served in the military for eight years and talks about her service with pride. She left the Air Force because she never received the training in linguistics. She was honorably discharged and pursued full-time study following discharge.

Because of her limited income, she lived with a number of other students in rented housing. She was older than the other undergraduates and grew weary of their behavior. In her senior year, she learned of an efficiency apartment which was available near the university that she could afford. The landlord informed her that the rent was low because a woman had previously died in the apartment and no one was willing to rent it. Karen assumed that the woman's death was an unfortunate circumstance that created an opportunity to get into a quieter living situation. She moved into the apartment, happy to have both quiet and privacy. After several weeks, she began to find that she was becoming ill.

After an examination at the student health center, she was told that she most likely had mononucleosis, which is not uncommon on university campuses. After a few weeks, she became increasingly tired and low energy. She sought out other medical advice. While she was undergoing further testing, it was reported in the news that an agricultural pesticide was being used by the owner of several apartments in the area as an insecticide. The apartment complex Karen lived in was one of those treated with this agricultural product. This chemical exposure led to Karen's diagnosis of Chronic Fatigue Immune Deficiency Syndrome.

Karen's grades plummeted. She worked with an academic advisor who assisted in negotiating with professors so that she could graduate as scheduled. Karen then moved to her mother's home and legal proceedings unfolded regarding the landlord's negligence.

Karen had found a physician who was supportive and helpful. It was recommended that she adjust her diet and take a regimen of various supplements as well as a low dosage of a commonly used SSRI. She needed to wait to see to what degree symptoms would remit.

Karen displays no suicidal ideation, nor the symptoms of a mood disorder. Yet, she states clearly that everything she was working for has been taken away from her and that she has nothing to live for.

Another aspect of the engaging dimension of her life was the need to return home to mother's care as an adult who has lived an independent life for fifteen years. For both Karen and her mother, this was a misordering of life and interrupted their developmental life patterns.

The Sociohistorical Dimension

Karen's sense of self was clearly related to her ethnic heritage as Native American. At the same time, based on her reported history, it was clear that she was raised at some distance from the intact culture of her tribe. While she learned some aspects of her culture from her family, she also explained that other aspects were things she has learned for herself, like the spoken language.

Karen framed the impact of her illness in a cultural context. She stated the people like her, who were no longer useful, would be left on the ice floe to die. That may be an accurate statement about her culture, but it is an incomplete one. For young people who suddenly became ill, there must also have been ceremonies and rituals for healing. Also, what process would have been involved in determining that it was time for someone to die on the ice? In her opening presentation, Karen has omitted these aspects of her culture from the discussion. Could this be symptomatic for Karen's loss of hope for the future? Is it a reflection of her limited knowledge about the culture? The therapeutic process needs to explore these gaps.

The sociohistorical dimension also includes the culture of her family. She reported that her father had a history of alcohol addiction which led to her parent's divorce. All of her siblings left home at age 18. Within her family life, there has been disruption. How does this history impact Karen's report of a not having connection with others? In what ways does this family history lead her to a strong sense of independence?

The Spiritual Dimension

A theme which is consistent with Karen is that if she has nothing to live for, then she has no reason to live. This theme is the articulation of how she has understood spirituality in her life: that the purpose of her life is to be useful. Her understanding of usefulness is connected to the sociohistorical dimension and the strong connection she experiences with her culture. She had entered the military to gain training in linguistics to be useful to Native American people. She left the military, which she reported liking, in order to pursue the life purpose of being useful to her people. A chronic physical illness has threatened her life purpose, resulting in her statement that she has nothing left to live for.

Other ways in which an individual may organize spirituality including particular practices or finding meaning in relationships or other aspects of life seem to be absent in Karen's life. She reports only one opening in this spiritual dimension: being useful to people of her culture. Without that, she is in essence reporting that she has nothing.

Considerations for Therapeutic Intervention

The role of a psychologist, counselor, or social worker is to enable a client to function as optimally as possible within the client's immediate world. For Karen, this will require some understanding of Chronic Fatigue Immune Deficiency Syndrome and how it impacts Karen. To that end, consultation with her physician is recommended.

No matter what the clinician's theoretical orientation, the model of the integrated self enables the clinician to more clearly identify the way in which aspects of Karen's culture are manifested in the way she has organized the spiritual dimension of her life. Karen consistently identified that being useful to people is significant to her. It will be helpful to Karen if a clinician could build on this connection and use it as a resource for helping her engage in activities, relationships, and other goals while dealing with physical limitations.

Clearly, Karen's former sense of self has been lost and she needs to grieve this loss. From that bereavement process, a new integration can arise. Karen's ability to integrate a new sense of self will be based on the importance she places on being useful to the people of her culture.

In my work with Karen, the concept of usefulness was an important metaphor. While her physical energy was limited, because she had access to the Internet, she was able to join online groups both for people with Chronic Fatigue Syndrome as well as those who were part of Native American groups. Karen was a very bright and determined individual. While we engaged in other therapeutic work on her self concept, she collected traditional Native American stories online from various tribes. Slowly, she created a website that catalogued the stories, making them available to people who did not have access to this lore. We explored how what she viewed as keeping herself from boredom when having sleepless nights was actually being useful to people whom she would never meet.

Fundamentally, the interventions used with Karen were cognitive-behavioral and Gestalt techniques within a framework of active listening and unconditional positive regard. What was different in the treatment was the understanding of the how the four dimensions of the self came together to play a significant part in Karen's life. It was by working toward greater integration of the four dimensions that Karen became a healthier individual.

The Case of Greg

Greg was a 38-year-old gay white man. He was completing a master's degree in social work and was an intern in a family and children agency. He had been in therapy before and was treated both for depression and for early childhood abuse.

While working at the internship site, Greg found himself overly attached to the children with whom he worked. He also experienced nightmares that regularly disturbed his sleep. Sometimes the dreams were about his childhood; other times they were about the abuse his client's experienced.

As a boy, Greg's father ritually took him to the basement and sexually abused him. These trips to the basement were framed as "discipline" for things like talking back to mother or not completing chores. Often mother would report an infraction to father. Later in the evening, father would take the boy to the basement and give him a choice between a belt whipping or sexual intercourse. This "discipline" began in early childhood and continued until Greg's adolescence when he was physically strong enough to stop his father from taking him to the basement.

Greg was concerned that the dreams and lack of resolution with the childhood abuse was interfering with his internship. His dream was to work with children. He saw that as his way of breaking the cycle of abuse that was part of his family.

Case Analysis Based on the Integrated Model of Self

Greg presented himself for therapy because he recognized from prior treatment that his traumatic memories were triggered by the stress of working with children. Because of success in prior treatment with other clinicians, Greg was open and motivated as a client but also concerned about what the sleep disturbances might mean for his career.

The Engaging Dimension

Greg recognized that the counter-transference with his clients and the dreams he was having were an indication that he needed therapeutic assistance. This presenting problem is focused in the engaging dimension of Greg's sense of self: he is not able to function the way he desires. Treatment goals center on resolving the traumatic memories so that Greg can resume day-to-day functioning.

It is not unusual for a new intern to lack sufficient professional boundaries to limit counter transference. Greg, like many new interns and therapists, wanted to save his clients from their situations. Greg's history of abuse made it difficult for him to establish healthy boundaries in many relationships. The current problem of engaging in appropriate ways as an intern was an extension of his traumatic family relationship.

The Embodied Dimension

Greg was having dreams that disturbed his sleep. He described that in some dreams he sees one or another of his clients being abused. Then the image faded into Greg's own abuse from his father. Other times, it is the reverse: the dream began with him as the victim of abuse from his father and morphed into a dream in which a client is abused. Because of these dreams, his sleep was not restorative. He was growing weary, eating irregular meals, and felt less and less focused when awake.

The Sociohistorical Dimension

Greg's family is one in which abuse was normative. He reported that the only times he experienced a sense of intimacy with his father was when he was taken to the basement. Otherwise, he stated that his father generally ignored him. He also stated that he did not experience a close connection with this mother. Greg was their only child.

As part of previous therapy, Greg confronted his parents about the abuse. He explained that his father denied the abuse occurred and his mother insisted that his purpose in making the accusation was to hurt them. For the last five years, the only contact Greg has had with his parents was a Christmas card.

A larger cultural issue for Greg was internalized stigmatization about being a gay man and working with children. While the profession of social work has clear ethical standards that sexual orientation should not be a source of bias, Greg had internalized negative views of homosexuality prevalent in American culture. He was not identified as gay at the internship site or in his graduate program because he feared that someone may try to stop him from working with children.

The Spiritual Dimension

As an older, non-traditional student, Greg had sacrificed a great deal to return to graduate school in order to fulfill a goal: to work with children. The goal had a redemptive quality about it: to work with abused children as a way of breaking the cycle of abuse both for them and for him. This goal gave the sacrifices he has made to pursue a graduate degree a certain meaning. More than this, by working with children, he hoped to create some sort of meaning out of his own abuse.

The energy in this pursuit is a way to create meaning, purpose or value in one's life, but it was a very dangerous way to do that. Pursuit of this goal can be dangerous to him and to the children with whom he worked.

Considerations for Therapeutic Intervention

As with other survivors of trauma, empowering Greg to return to a more stabile state is important. Working with Greg included rehearsing with him how to speak to his clinical supervisor about the experience of counter-transference. Greg was initially resistant because he did not want to identify himself as a gay man. His sexual orientation was not the issue; counter-transference was. Further work was also needed to help him create boundaries between self and work. To that end, I encouraged him to create a ritual for when he would leave the agency at the end of the day. He would drive to a nearby park to do a relaxation exercise. In that exercise, he placed his cares for the day on a large boulder that was located in the corner of a park and imagined that the boulder held the weight of his burdens.

Other aspects of clinical work with Greg included using an empty chair technique to continue the confrontation with his own parents as well as cognitive techniques to minimize the impact of irrational thoughts.

The spiritual dimension of work with Greg was of particular importance to me. Greg assigned a redemptive meaning to his work with abused children. It was his belief that if he could save children from abuse, then he would save himself. The value he assigned to working with abused children was, on the one hand, an irrational thought. On the other hand, it provided him with a great deal of energy and strong commitment for returning to graduate school at midlife. From this case, it is important to remember that something that has spiritual value can still present danger to an individual. While that danger is easier to see in cases of cult membership or in similar extremes, more common is the danger that can be present from an unhealthy pursuit of meaning or purpose in life.

Aligning myself with Greg, I affirmed his goal to work with children as something positive but encouraged him to consider ways he could work with children that did not require direct client services, but could include program development, fundraising, education, or advocacy. As he began to see that he could help children in many ways that did not require direct services, I then began to explore with him the ways in which he needed to save himself from his own history of abuse. From this, we were able to explore his experience of loneliness and alien-ation. I encouraged him to participate in a social group with other gay men and lesbians. He began to attend a church-based social support group that, in addition to an informal self-help discussion, had regular social activities. This provided a forum in which Greg could be himself and establish friendships that maintained healthy boundaries. It also led him to consider other ways he could find a sense of fulfillment in life by having friends and possibly developing a long term relationship. Maintaining friends and dating were problematic areas for Greg. Because of his history of shattered boundaries from abuse, he would often push to get too close to others very early in relationships. Again, the issues of boundaries became an important part of the work with Greg.

Within a few weeks, the dreams faded. Greg had the wisdom to continue in therapy for several months and to continue close work with his clinical supervisor. At the end of the internship, Greg was offered a job at the agency where he worked for several years.

The Therapeutic Approach

In the two cases analyzed, the integrated model of self was the basis for assessment and treatment planning. It is important to note that the integrated model of self was used with commonly accepted interventions. What makes these case studies fundamentally different from mental health services commonly provided in many clinical settings is the fundamental approach that understands cultures as an integral part of the self and spirituality as the integral motivation for therapeutic movement.

Spirituality is the integral motivate for therapeutic movement because it is the dimension of self that draws the individual to aspire to something "more than" what is already apparent or apprehended in day to day life. This aspiration to greater meaning, purpose, or value is an animating principle that empowers change and growth.

In both clients presented, the issues rooted in the sociohistorical dimension shaped their identity were recognized as part of the overall process of development and growth toward wholeness.

Ultimately, the integrated model of self challenges clinicians to understand the client in a more complex and holistic manner. It is from this integrated perspective that clinicians can employ their skills as experts in the engaging dimension of self to support the client to become "more than" the client has been.

Chapter 5

Approaches to Spiritual Assessment

Joe is a 47-year-old white man. He has been attending Alcoholics Anonymous for nine or ten months. Meeting with a clinician for the first time, he explains, "The program has been very helpful. It took me a few weeks to stop drinking, but after doing 30 meetings in 30 days, I've been sober. I have a great home group and talk with my sponsor several times a week. But I'm confused about AA as a spiritual program. I still don't know what that means. My sponsor and my home group are like higher powers to me because they've done it. I don't think I'm a spiritual person. I don't go to church. I don't pray. I really just don't know what this spirituality stuff is all about. It must be important because everyone at the meetings talks about it.

It is a very simple principle in the practice of psychology: to include a dimension of a person's experience as part of a treatment plan, that dimension of experience must be assessed. Without an initial assessment and a later assessment to determine the level of change, a therapist cannot evaluate the effectiveness of treatment.

The foundation of an assessment is the existence of norms, constructs, or definitions describing the object assessed. An assessment can be as simple as asking a client to quantify the level of an emotion on a scale from one to five. Because of ongoing assessment, a therapist can chart the progression of a therapeutic process. Assessment is a particularly challenging issue in terms of spirituality because there are no mutually understood norms, constructs, or definitions for spirituality or spiritual experience. A lack of definition further complicates issues of validity and reliability for assessment. In general, the professional expectation of an assessment process or tool is that it will measure what it purports to measure and will provide a reliable result. Although several measures demonstrate reliability, it's important to know what these measures validly measure because the operationalized definition of spirituality can vary a great deal among assessment tools.

Spiritual assessment began to emerge as a practice in hospice care. Chaplains, social workers or other members of the hospice team assessed spirituality through the use of structured interviews. This approach is very subjective and often produces several pages of notes in a patient's chart Such assessments included history of religious or spiritual practices, the current state of these practices, and discussion of how beliefs influence end of life planning. Cornelius J. Van Der Poel presents a very thorough model for this approach to spiritual assessment in the 1998 book *Sharing the Journey: Spiritual Assessment and Pastoral Response to Persons with Incurable Illnesses*. A second approach to spiritual assessment is the use of specific, closed ended questions about spirituality and religion on in-take or assessment forms. This method is sometimes used by physicians in private practice as well as by health care institutions. The American College of Physicians published this type of assessment in 1999. This assessment recommended the use of four basic questions: (1) "Is faith (religion, spirituality) important to you in this illness?" (2) "Has faith been important to you at other times in your life?" (3) "Do you have someone to talk to about religious matters?" and (4) "Would you like to explore religious matters with someone?" (Lo, 1999).

The first approach to spiritual assessment provides extensive information that is very subjective. Most clients experience an hour spent on spiritual assessment as a waste of time because it is not clear how the information is useful for treatment. An hour spent specifically for spiritual assessment is also not practical for a clinician because of the limited time available for clinical care. While the second approach is more practical, the assessment asks closed ended questions. By asking whether one has someone to talk to or would want someone to talk to about religious or spiritual matters, the underlying assumption is that this information is not particularly relevant to treatment.

In the United States, the Joint Commission (formerly the Joint Commission for the Accreditation of Healthcare Organizations) requires that spiritual assessment be included in the standard care at the institutions it accredits. The Joint Commission does not stipulate how assessment should be done and leaves this task to the organization. This demonstrates wisdom by the Joint Commission. Spirituality cannot be assessed in a standard way. Nor can an assessment tool developed in one institution be used effectively in another. Instead, it is vital that clinicians consider what role spirituality is likely to play in the treatment of clients and develop assessment strategies based on the unique client population and treatment provided.

In developing an approach to spiritual assessment for a particular clinical setting, it is important to consider what kind of information is most helpful for the services provided. For example, in the context of crisis management, it may be important to ask if it would be helpful to have someone with whom the client can discuss religious or spiritual matters. On the other hand, for longer term treatment, obtaining a clear history of the client's religious and spiritual resources may be valuable. For research or for treatment in institutional settings, an objective, quantified approach to spiritual assessment is often more valuable than a subjective, qualitative approach.

In whatever approach to spiritual assessment is used, the constructs of spirituality or religion must be carefully operationalized in order to obtain valid and relevant information from clients. Clients from various age groups or cultures may not understand what is meant by the word spirituality. On the other hand, the practice of religion can be equally limiting. Further, there are practices that are not labeled as religious or spiritual but may sustain a person's inner spirit. Examples can include sitting in silence while doing needlework or jogging at a regular time each day. While the client may view these activities as a hobby or exercise, the activities can also have the place a role in the client's life that is similar to a traditional spiritual practice, like praying a rosary.

A Spiritual History

There several approaches to a spiritual history. One common type of spiritual history is asking a client a series of proscribed questions as is done in other kinds of psycho-social histories. Maugan (1996) developed a 32-item questionnaire as a spiritual history. Examples of questions from this tool include:

"Do you have a spiritual life that is important to you?

Describe the beliefs and practices of your religion that you personally accept.

Describe those beliefs and practices that you do not accept or follow.

Do you belong to any religious or spiritual groups or communities?

What lifestyle activities or practices does your religion encourage, discourage or forbid?"

This kind of spiritual history can be added to existing psychosocial in-take interviews with a great deal of success.

Within the context of therapy itself, there are techniques that are viewed as congruent with the therapeutic process that can be used to take a spiritual history. One example is a genogram. A client can be invited to trace religion and spiritual issues as part of this multi-generational family diagram. Doing so can provide both insight into the family history of spirituality. It also opens the exploration of how the client is presently similar to and different from others in the family regarding issues of spirituality and religion.

I developed a process for taking a spiritual history some years ago and which I ask clients to complete as homework. The instructions are relatively simple. Clients are asked to create a time line of significant events in their lives by drawing a line on a sheet of paper, marking one end with the client's birth date and the other end with the current date. The client is asked to list any events the client views as significant. Clients should not list events not viewed as significant despite social conventions associated with the event.

After completing this time line of significant events, clients are asked to use a second piece of paper to create a similar line listing significant spiritual experiences. The client defines spirituality in any way that is helpful to the client, as was done earlier in this book.

Once the client has completed both time lines, the time lines are discussed in session with a focus on looking at patterns that may emerge and how the client understands spirituality as playing a role in the client's life. For example, during particularly difficult times in life, a client may report having a series of several significant spiritual experiences because spirituality somehow supported the client through the difficult time. For another client, during difficult times in life, there may be an absence of spiritual experience. This client may report believing that God had abandoned or was punishing the client. Such a history provides insights about the way spirituality functions within the client's life and how beliefs are understood in very practical ways.

Spiritual Assessments

The difference between a spiritual history and a spiritual assessment is that a spiritual history tracks the role of spirituality in an individual's life over time whereas a spiritual assessment is aimed at the present role of spirituality in an individual's life.

One approach to spiritual assessment as an interview that is particularly noteworthy is a tool developed by faculty members at Brown University's School of Medicine called the Hope Questionnaire. Based on the mnemonic, H.O.P.E., the assessment addresses significant dimensions of a patient's spirituality in the content of health care.

H – Sources of hope, meaning, comfort:
   (1) What are your sources of hope, meaning, comfort, strength, peace, love and connection?
   (2) What do you hold onto during difficult times?
   (3) What sustains you and keeps you going?
O – Organized Religion
   (1) Are your part of a religious or spiritual community? Does it help you? How?
   (2) What aspects of your religion are helpful to you and not so helpful to you?
P – Personal spirituality and practices
   (1) Do you have any personal spiritual beliefs that are independent of organized religion?
   (2) What aspect of your spirituality or spiritual practices do you find most helpful to you personally?
E – Effects on medical care and end-of-life issues
   (1) Has being sick affected your ability to do things that usually help you spiritually?
   (2) As a doctor, is there anything that I can do to help you access the resources that usually help you?
   (3) Are there any specific practices or restrictions I should know about in providing your medical care?

The questions are sufficiently specific while also allowing the patient to operationalize the construct "spirituality" in a way that is appropriate for the patient. In addition, by rewording the section on medical care to refer to mental health services, this assessment tool can be used in mental health settings.

The Fetzer Institute has developed the most exhaustive work on spiritual assessment. After funding a number of studies on spiritual assessment to develop appropriate tools, the Fetzer Institute published the *Multidimensional Measurement of Religiousness/Spirituality for Use in Health Research*. This publication, available on the website of the Fetzer Institute, contains twelve different assessments on religion and spirituality that operationalize these constructs in a variety of ways. In addition, the publication contains the *Brief Multidimension Measurement of Religiousness/Spirituality* that uses items from various other surveys to provide a brief, composite assessment tool.

The work produced by Fetzer, which is ongoing, is significant not just for health related research but also as a resource for those engaged in the development of spiritual assessment tools and processes within mental health settings. The work is nothing less than invaluable for clinicians and researchers interested in spiritual assessment.

While many institutions and agencies quickly adopt spiritual assessment strategies in order to meet the requirements of certification or funding, a more prudent strategy is to provide training to staff about the relationship of spirituality to service provision. As clinicians and agencies develop greater awareness of spirituality and spiritual assessment, effective strategies can be developed to meet the needs of the specific population of clients served and the services provided.

The clinician listens to Joe's concerns about spirituality. She asks some questions to clarify his involvement in the twelve-step program and how it has fit into his life. From his report, she concludes that he has learned a great deal about himself from the program and is maintaining sobriety. She begins to assess what spirituality may mean for him. "Joe," she begins, "From what you've told me about your life and recovery, you've been through a great deal. When you faced hard times, what kept you going? What got your through?" By incorporating questions from the HOPE instrument, the clinician begins to map sources of spirituality in Joe's life. Based on that information, she will develop goals and a treatment plan to enable Joe to identify the ways spirituality operates in his life.

Chapter 6

Current Research on Spirituality and Mental Health

The presentation was going smoothly. The participants were attentive and engaged. Before lunch, the group discussed the definition of spirituality, learned about the integrated model of the self, and analyzed case studies. As we came back for lunch, I reviewed some key points to get us back on focus and raised a couple of questions for discussion. It was then that a gentleman in the back of the room asked, "I understand that spirituality is important to you in your work. But it's something that wasn't part of my training. While what you're saying is appealing, I'm not convinced it has a place in therapy. It seems to me like you're imposing a framework on clients just because it appeals to you."

The challenge raised by this seasoned clinician is not new to me. When I began to study spirituality thirty years ago, his argument had substantive merit. At that time, to consider an approach that integrated spirituality with psychology seemed to be based on personal religious or metaphysical beliefs. Over the last ten years, a great deal of research on the relationship between spirituality and psychology, neurology, and treatment outcomes has occurred. The pattern of research is consistent: spirituality plays an important role in mental health and positive treatment outcomes. It's not just metaphysics; it's evidence-based. While it is not the goal of this chapter to provide an exhaustive review of literature on the integration of spirituality and psychology, it is important to draw highlights from the evidence that supports and clarifies the role of spirituality in mental health. Research on this topic has evolved over the last decade and has developed greater specificity. Of course, as some research questions are answered, more questions continue to emerge.

The movement toward an evidence-based understanding of the role of spirituality and mental health became apparent with the 1998 publication of Dr. Harold G. Koenig's landmark text, *The Handbook of Religion and Mental Health.* Beginning with historical foundations and the etiology of mental disorders as understood in various religious traditions, Koenig considered the practices of psychiatry and psychology and the role of religion and spirituality in stress management, coping, depression, anxiety, substance abuse and recovery, and psychosis. The early research summarized in this text supported the notion that spirituality and religious practice had a generally positive role in the treatment of mental disorders. Based on this research, Koenig considered the integration of religious belief within the context of the provision of therapeutic intervention.

While *The Handbook of Religion and Mental Health* is a landmark text and laid a foundation for an evidence-based approach for the integration of psychology and spirituality, its approach suggests that clinicians understand the beliefs and nuances of different religious traditions to be competent clinicians. In other words, knowledge of Islam, Buddhism, or a specific indigenous belief system is needed to work with a client who adheres to that particular belief system. Much like early literature in the cultural competence movement, which supposed that a clinician must understand a particular culture to work with an individual from that culture, this approach is inadequate because each person organizes both cultural identity and spirituality in a unique way. This is true even when the person is an adherent to a religious tradition. Formal beliefs and practices are mixed with personal beliefs and practices. With the rise of globalization, the beliefs and practices of individuals are often drawn from multiple sources. For example, a suburban mother may be an active member of a particular church because the church sponsors a reputable daycare program for working mothers. In addition to attending Sunday services, she also belongs to a health club and finds classes in yoga and tai chi beneficial. Each year, on her birthday, she visits a psychic for a Tarot card reading. In other words, while an active member of a Christian church, she also engages in Hindu, Taoist, and esoteric practices not associated with Christianity. Assuming that because the woman attends a particular church each Sunday that she only ascribes to the beliefs and practices of that institution would be incorrect. The implication for both clinicians and researchers is that spirituality must be viewed in broader terms than adherence to religion or a particular spiritual tradition. Much like the development of cross-cultural counseling that has led to models of cultural competence that can be employed with clients no matter their background and the ways they have enculturated particular values, spirituality needs to be understood in a holistic and integrative manner. This has led to the investigation of the role of beliefs systems and spiritual experiences on mental health and neurology.

Koenig and early researchers were helpful in establishing an important foundation for the inclusion of spirituality in the treatment of specific disorders. A review of research from the last five years finds much greater specificity in the research than existed just ten or fifteen years ago.

Early research supported the positive role of spirituality as mental health treatment. As research evolved, inquiry has considered whether all forms of spirituality positively correlate with mental health outcomes. Other lines of research consider when spirituality and spiritual practices are most helpful.

Is Spirituality Always Positive?

Those who support an integrative approach of spirituality with mental health and health care appear to assert implicitly that spirituality and spiritual practice always play a positive role within an individual's life. Such an assumption is simplistic. Not only have spiritual writers throughout the generations and across traditions asserted that there are illuminating aspects of spirituality as well as experiences that reflect what may be disconcerting aspects of spirituality, so too contemporary research indicates that spirituality can function in positive ways that enhance health and well-being as well as negative ways that diminish health and well-being.

While beliefs about the nature of a deity shape the meditative experience as something positive for mental health treatment not potentially negative, so too does the orientation of belief and practice. Research by Baetz and Toews (2009) describe two categories of religious and spiritual expression: intrinsic and extrinsic. An intrinsic orientation to religion and spirituality, which organizes beliefs and practices based on internalized beliefs that supports a sense of personal security and empowerment, leads to a decrease in depressive symptoms and an increase in overall mental health attributes. Conversely, an extrinsic orientation to religion and spirituality, which focuses on status in relationship to a deity and self-justification, leads to increased depression and a decrease in overall mental health attributes and coping. An extrinsic orientation to religion is often based on a schema of a punitive deity.

Similarly, Kohl's research (2009) has distinguished between positive and negative spiritual experiences. In spiritual experiences, people often report a sense of a loss of self or stepping outside of self. Individuals who hold belief systems that help to interpret spiritual experiences or provide a context for explaining the dynamics of spiritual experiences often find this loss of self as a positive sign. Those without a framework for understanding the experience may become fearful, anxious, or avoidant. When a spiritual experience is unknown, incomprehensible, or unfamiliar, the result is increased anxiety, fear, or self-doubt. It is not surprising that for those who have a negative or fearful description of spiritual experience, stress increases. Conversely, for those who describe spiritual experience in positive terms, the experience is stress reducing.

Finally, it is unclear how many people have experienced psychological, sexual, or physical abuse related to involvement in a religious or spiritual group. While pedophilia among clergy or obedience to cult leaders can be found in news headlines, many people have experienced manipulation, fraud, or other harm through association with various groups, teachers, or clergy. While research is not available on the frequency of abusive experiences, individuals who have been victims of abuse may find it difficult to sort out religious and spiritual experience or its role in life. This is true for both identifiable victims, as in someone raped by a member of the clergy, or members of specific groups often ostracized by religious organizations, including women, gay men and lesbians.

The Potency of Meditation

Benson's (1975) pioneering medical research demonstrated the role of relaxation in stress reduction. Various breathing techniques, visualization, and meditation can be helpful in the treatment of mood disorders and anxiety disorders. Since 1975, meditation has become the most researched spiritual practice. Research indicates the meditation plays a very important role in brain health resulting in numerous benefits for mental health. Neurological research by Andrew Newberg has led to the discovery that the images that are part of visualization or meditation greatly influence both mood and anxiety disorders. Among Newberg's findings are that the beliefs surrounding meditation are related to the impact meditation has on the practitioner. Those who hold an image of a deity that is loving, compassionate, and forgiving experience a reduction of stress, depressive symptoms, and generalized anxiety. Such individuals also experience an increase in feelings of love, compassion, and security. Conversely, practitioners of meditation who believe in a deity that is authoritarian may have an increase in anxiety. It is important to note that research by the Baylor Institute for the Study of Religion (2006) has found that 23% of Americans hold a belief in a benevolent god, while 31% view god as authoritarian; 24% as distant; and 16% as critical. In other research, Newberg reports that particular meditation practices can delay or slow the progression of Alzheimer's disease and other forms of dementia. By engaging in a daily meditation practice that includes both verbal repetition and tactile stimulus, mechanisms in the brain slow the progression of dementia over time. Meditation is also a helpful strategy in trauma recovery. All life experiences modify the brain in some way. This is referred to as neural plasticity. Trauma and traumatic memory can modify the brain in ways that keep the traumatic memory reactive. This can result in the atrophication of brain cells. The practice of meditation over time has the ability to support the natural function of the limbic system and the characteristics of neural plasticity to enable the integration of traumatic memory on the neural level. In some cases, new neural pathways can develop over atrophied areas.In general, the benefits of meditation are found with a regular or daily practice. In addition to the mental health benefits of meditation, there is also an extensive body of research on the health benefits of meditation. This spiritual practice found within every major religious tradition and practiced today outside of religious contexts, offers tremendous support for general health and mental health benefit whether the practice is associated with religious belief or as a practice of inner quiet.

Role of Spirituality in the Treatment

Treatment for any mental disorder typically follows a progression of stages. At each stage, tasks and goals emerge and evolve requiring that the client to utilize different resources to support recovery. Within the evolution of the treatment process, do clients use spiritual resources differently based on the progression of the treatment?

When examining treatment for depression, Sorajjakool (2008) found that the role of spirituality does evolve over the course of treatment. When initially presenting for treatment, depression creates the experience of disconnection from self, from others, and from God. At this time, clients often report of loss of spiritual connection or an ability to use spiritual resources that are typically a source of strength or comfort. However, in early treatment, spirituality can play a role in coping. Based on one's belief system, there can be an openness to find solutions to personal problems like depression that provide a basis for coping skills. Later in treatment, as a client begins to analyze the patterns, schemas, and experience of depression, spirituality can be foundational as the client explores a sense of meaning within the depression itself. The depressed individual, looking to make sense out of the experience, often yearns for meaning or purpose that can be addressed through a belief system. By organizing a sense of meaning for the illness and for self, the client begins to move out of the experience of depression toward a growing experience of recovery. The foundational dimension of spirituality as the source for meaning and purpose in life can be key to the movement from depression to a healthy sense of self.

In study of individuals with bipolar disorder and schizophrenia, Lukoff (2007) adapted a twelve-step recovery model for the treatment of those with persistent mental disorders. The adaptation of the twelve-step model included particular features. Research participants were educated about recovery as a spiritual journey. The participants were encouraged to be involved with a spiritual path or religious community based on the client's beliefs and value system. Regular use of spiritual practices from the participants' chosen spiritual path or religious community was encouraged. They were also encouraged to seek advice from appropriate spiritual leaders. Participants were asked to model their spirituality to others in appropriate ways in group settings. Lukoff's analysis (2007) of the use of the twelve-step model found that clients benefited from this model by the ability to use spiritual resources as a way to support coping. Among those resources was church attendance, which increased the level of the client's social and emotional support. Spirituality increased the individual's sense of wholeness while living with persistent mental disorders. While further research in this area is warranted, it appears that the role of spirituality as a resource for therapeutic work takes on different qualities over the course of treatment.

Spirituality and Resiliency

Over the last five years, extensive research has been conducted on the role of resiliency and treatment and recovery. The data is very consistent: a strong positive correlation exists between spirituality and resiliency. Studies examine a wide variety of topics, including: children's beliefs and emotional well-bring (Eaude, 2009); adjustment and psychological distress among urban adolescents (Van Dyke, 2009); refugees resettled in a new country (Sossou, 2008); surviving in the midst of workplace adversity (Jackson, 2007); and general mental health for the elderly (Langer, 2004).

In a meta-analysis of forty-nine studies on spirituality, religious belief and resiliency following traumatic incidence, Peres, et al. (2007) found that belief systems that provided a meaningful interpretation of traumatic experience showed a positive correlation between spirituality and resiliency. However, there was also a clear negative correlation between belief systems that led to doubt or further questioning and resilience. In other words, when following a traumatic experience, if an individual's belief is that a deity was punishing them or when an individual repeatedly asks, "Why is God doing this to me?" then there is a decline in physical and mental health.

Research on resiliency that considers the type of belief system held by an individual appears to parallel the research on meditation and other practices: positive and empowering belief systems lead to increased resiliency whereas beliefs in a harsh, judgment, fickle or punitive deity can lead to further decompensation.

Spiritual Fitness and the Military

The importance of spirituality as a distinct domain from the psychological dimension of the individual has taken on critical importance within the United States Military. Based on a review of research on the role of spirituality in maintaining overall mental health as well as supporting recovery, the military understands spiritual fitness as a key element to operational readiness for troops. The importance of spiritual fitness for the military can be summarized by this statement: "Spiritual fitness is key to ensuring optimal force readiness and protection and enhancing resilience and recovery following combat-related trauma" (Hufford, 2010). To that end, greater emphasis is developing within the military for inclusion of spiritual fitness as a factor in readiness.

Conclusion

In considering the breadth of research on spirituality and mental health, two important factors emerge. First, spirituality plays an important role in mental health and treatment outcomes. Because of this, mental health professions need to develop competency in addressing spirituality and its role within a person's life. Second, while spirituality plays an important role in mental health, positive belief systems have the ability to enhance mental health. Belief systems focused on in a punitive, harsh deity lead to the decompensation of mental health. Therefore, a simplistic view of spirituality as somehow always positive is not warranted.

Because clinicians want to avoid imposing their beliefs on a client, clinicians rarely challenge religious beliefs that are detrimental to clients. This does not serve the best interest of the client. Instead, clinicians need to develop the skills needed to examine belief systems and challenge aspects that lead to an increase in depression, anxiety, or failure to recover from trauma. Successful approaches for challenging such belief systems parallel the therapeutic interventions used in the challenging of self-defeating thoughts and behaviors in clinical settings.

In response to the question from the clinician, I began to discuss some of the research on the relationship between spirituality and clinical outcomes. I watched as many participants became more animated. I asked participants if they had experience integrating spirituality or spiritual practices with clients. The discussion grew into a very lively exchange with clinicians sharing a wide variety of cases in which spirituality played an important role.

"Based on what I've heard, I have two questions," I stated as a summary. "First, how can we, as individual practitioners, augment our theoretical orientation to clinical work to better include spirituality? Second, what further training is needed to address spirituality with our clients in more competent ways?"

Chapter 7

Ethical Considerations for Integrating Spirituality and Mental Health Practice

Dr. Sophia has worked with women who are survivors of physical and sexual abuse and assault for more than twenty years. A noted expert in the field, she has stayed current with research on traumatic memory and the brain. She incorporates techniques like EMDR and meditation as part of treatment because of their positive benefits in resolving trauma. While working with a new client, Rose, Dr. Sophia taught a simple technique for meditation and asked Rose to use it 20 minutes each day. Following the meditation, she was to journal for ten minutes. Dr. Sophia also began each session with ten minutes of silent meditation. She explained that this would better enable Rose to "speak the truth of her soul." Rose found that the time in meditation was opening her to feelings and memories she had not recognized in the past. She also began to feel more and more attached to Dr. Sophia and told all of her friends about her new meditation partner: Dr. Sophia. When Rose shared with Dr. Sophia how important their friendship was and how much she appreciated the time in meditation, Dr. Sophia suggested that she attend a workshop with other women on spirituality. Rose got the information and made plans to attend the workshop. When Rose arrived for the daylong event, she was pleased to find that Dr. Sophia, dressed in a flowing white robe, was the facilitator. As she talked with other women that day, she discovered that many of the women were current or former clients of Dr. Sophia. Following the workshop, Rose went home frustrated. In her meditation journal, she began to write about the resentment she had in sharing her friend, Dr. Sophia, with other women.

Overarching all work done in the practice of psychology is the ethical mandate to do no harm. Based on the Hippocratic Oath, as modern day healers of mental disorders, it is our responsibility to work with clients in a way that benefits the client within the client's immediate world. The challenge of ethics has become more complex as communities have grown to be multicultural. While the integrated model presented in this text enables us to understand the role of culture in the development of the self in a more comprehensive way, consideration of the spiritual dimension of the self adds a complex dimension of diversity to consider in therapy.

While the ethical codes of conduct from the multiple mental health professions vary in specific content, the general principles among the professions are consonant with each other. Rather than citing how each ethical code reflects specifics issues to related to spirituality and clinical practice, consideration will focus on several key ethical issues within the professional practice of mental health..

Values and the Spiritual Dimension

Inclusion of the spiritual dimension of the integrated self as part of the therapeutic process raises certain assumptions about values. One value is that personal growth and integration is of benefit for people withunderlying values on which the model is based. Another value is that all four dimensions of an individual's experience are valuable. These values are based on the assumption made in a therapeutic process: the improved functioning in life is valued and to be supported. From this perspective, all therapeutic work maintains a basis in values. To be free of values in therapy or for a therapist to prevent personal values from entering clinical work is not an option because the nature of the work itself is based on particular values. Simply, professionals working in the application of psychology assume that it is better live in a way that most supports optimal functioning.

While the nature of therapeutic intervention itself is based on the value that improved functioning is better for people, the focus of clinical work is the client's experience. Because of that, it is important to keep the therapeutic relationship free from the clinician's experience because of the ways that can lead to bias. The desire to maintain this basic ethic which relates to limits of self-disclosure often results in agency regulations that religion and spirituality should never be addressed. Such policies are short sighted and do more to limit the client than they do in preventing practices that may be viewed as unethical. For example, just as a skilled clinician can address a client's experience of depression without delving into the clinician's own experience of the same disorder, so too can the role the client's spirituality plays in the client's life be explored without the clinician setting becoming a place for the clinician to inappropriately disclose beliefs, practices, experiences, and personal integration of the spiritual dimension of life.

Assessment and the Spiritual Dimension

In a previous chapter, various methods of spiritual assessment were considered. While the Joint Commission requires that spiritual assessments be completed as part of the care provided in all of the facilities it accredits, specific elements of a spiritual assessment are not required. Instead, individual organizations define the content and scope of spiritual assessment. This reflects a very important ethical issue for assessment: information asked by a provider should reasonably be part of the client's care plan. In other words, while some level of spiritual assessment is generally appropriate, it is not appropriate to ask for information that will not be related to the treatment received.

By asking about certain aspects of a client's life, an expectation is raised that the information provided will be useful for treatment. For example, asking about the role of family rituals in a client's life will probably not provide useable information about the client in a crisis intervention center. However, in long term treatment for recovery of abuse or addiction, such information may be appropriate.

Because of this, caution should be taken in adopting spiritual assessment tools which have been developed for other settings. Review the assessment carefully to decide if the information likely to be obtained from each item of the assessment will be helpful to the general care provided in that particular setting. Determining how information gained can be used within the kinds of treatment provided in a particular setting moves assessment toward an ethically grounded process.

Dual Relationships

In all of the professions related to the practice of psychology, there are clear ethical codes that address the problem of dual relationships: having another kind of relationship with a client other than a therapeutic one. The underlying principle is that the therapeutic relationship is oriented toward the client's needs rather than the clinicians. To that end, while other kinds of relationships are good in themselves, being friends, colleagues, or dating clients is generally viewed as unethical.

Based on this principle, it is also important to keep the therapeutic relationship focused on the therapeutic process. In the general practice of psychology today, the therapeutic process is oriented toward a client meeting goals for change which lead to better functioning. Once those goals are met, the therapeutic relationship is terminated.

This process can become complicated when a dual relationship is initiated within the therapeutic setting. It is not uncommon for spiritually-based or religious-based clinicians to blur the relationship through the inclusion of spiritual or religious practices as part of therapy.

Consider the case of a small church pastor who practices and teaches meditations techniques. Suppose that the pastor of this small church was also a clinical social worker who was on staff at a counseling agency in another town. When working with a client, the pastor/social worker needs to be clear that the role is as clinician and not as pastor or spiritual teacher. This means that the clinical work must be oriented to achieving the goals of the treatment plan. While the client may learn that the social worker is also the pastor of a church and that the social worker leads a meditation group at that church, it raises an ethical concern for the pastor/social worker to encourage the client's participation in the church served by the pastor or in the meditation group.

There are times when it is clear a client could benefit the use of a spiritual practice. However, when working with a client, teaching that practice is only appropriate to the degree to which it supports the client's process in achieving the goals of the treatment plan. This boundary is clearly demonstrated in Jon Kabat-Zinn's Mindfulness-Based Stress Reduction. Techniques of mindfulness meditation are used by Kabat-Zinn and others as part of an overall therapeutic strategy. This is different from teaching mindfulness meditation as a spiritual practice in itself. Teaching a spiritual practice for the sake of the spiritual practice itself steps out of the therapeutic framework, even when the client is interested in learning the practice.

Many spiritually-based or religiously-based clinicians engage in meditation, Bible study, prayer and other spiritual practices with therapy. The ethical concern is that by doing so, the clinician blurs the boundaries of the role of therapist and establishes a dual relationship as spiritual teacher, guide or pastor within the therapeutic setting. This often delays termination and leads to clients who want to remain in therapy because the therapist has become their spiritual teacher, prayer partner or pastor.

It is the clinician's ethical responsibility that the therapeutic relationship remains free of a dual relationship by making sure that spiritual practices introduced in therapy are used for one purpose: achieving the goals established in the treatment plan.

Referrals to Spiritual and Religious Resources

When issues of spirituality become more focused in the clinical setting, clients may express a desire to explore spiritual practices or practices related to religion beyond the clinical work. In addition, there may be reasons within the treatment plan when it would be helpful to refer a client to specific spiritual resources. For example, there is a body of growing research that demonstrates that a regular practice of meditation is helpful in the treatment of PTSD, depression, and other mental disorders. While some clinicians may be able to teach helpful meditation techniques, recommending that a client maintain a regular practice will probably mean that the client will need additional support for that practice. This is no different from speaking to a client about weight loss without providing appropriate recommendations as to how weight loss can be addressed.

Just as clinicians maintain referral lists for other specializations, it is a necessary practice to develop referral sources to specialists in the area of spirituality. Like other referrals, it is the clinician's responsibility to determine the quality of service a client will receive. Establishing appropriate referral lists can be challenging, especially for resources outside of the clinician's own belief system.

Some recommendations that can be helpful in developing referral lists are: speaking to health care chaplains who are trained to work in ecumenical or interfaith settings; spiritual directors; staff members at retreat centers; established centers for spirituality and spiritual practice. Inquire about the training standards within a person's tradition and whether the person has met or exceeded those standards.

The professional group, Spiritual Directors International, provides an online directory of trained and certified spiritual directors around the world who can be of assistance in providing direct spiritual care to clients as well as help to educate clinicians about the resources in a particular community.

Cultural Competence and Spirituality

A growing body of literature is emerging on the significant role of spirituality as related to cultural competence in the practice of psychology. Contemporary theorists in psychology including Thomas A. Parham, Patricia Arredondo, and Eduardo Duran have written about the role of spirituality in culturally competent therapy for people of African descent, Latino/Hispanic, and indigeneous peoples. The general position taken by these writers is that to ignore spirituality when working with people from these racial or cultural groups is to fail to provide culturally competent therapy.

The model of the development of a culturally competent approach to therapy, based in the work of Derald Wing Sue and David Sue, looks at a developmental progression of awareness, knowledge and skills. While clearly each individual from a particular cultural or racial group is unique, the integrated model of self provides unique insights for engaging in ethical and culturally competent therapy which includes the spiritual dimension of the client. However, it would be naïve to consider this model sufficient in itself for culturally competent therapy because it suffers from the same limitation of other models in Western psychology: it values the integrated self as the primary source of identity. Such models are less helpful to individuals from collectivist cultures where the primary identity is in family, clan, or other social group. While the integrated model of the self does provide greater inclusion of the role of culture and cultural values for spirituality, it does so regarding the bias placed on the importance of the self as an independent entity from the social context.

When utilizing an integrated model for care in mental health, the focus of services provided and the professional relationship needs to be based on the ethical codes of the clinician's mental health profession. Because spirituality is sometimes viewed as a strength and positive value, ethical violations may inadvertently occur based on the attempt of providing holistic and integrated care. All mental health professions require a level of competence in providing services to client. This requirement remains true for the inclusion of spirituality in the provision of mental health services.

Dr. Patterson is another clinician who has worked with women who are survivors of physical and sexual abuse and assault for more than twenty years. A noted expert in the field, she has stayed current with research on traumatic memory and the brain. She incorporates techniques like EMDR and meditation as part of treatment because of their positive benefits in resolving trauma. While working with a new client, Jennifer, Dr. Patterson taught a simple technique for meditation and asked Jennifer to use it 20 minutes each day. Following the meditation, she was to journal for ten minutes. Dr. Patterson also began each session with a brief check-in process which included a two or three minutes of silence. Dr. Patterson explained the process to Jennifer and said that it's often easier for people to talk about difficult things when more relaxed and focused. Dr. Patterson also made it clear that if any part of the process was uncomfortable that Jennifer is free to talk about it and that the process can be changed. Jennifer found that the time in meditation was opening her to feelings and memories she hadn't recognized in the past. She also began to feel more attached to Dr. Patterson. Dr. Patterson sensed the transference and, near the end of a session one day, suggested that they talk about the therapeutic progress. Dr. Patterson asked Jennifer to assess her progress and sense of the course of therapy. Dr. Patterson reflected what Jennifersaid and closed the summary by saying, "Of course, what I want most is to help you to meet your goals in therapy and enable you to live a full and healthy life without therapy. I'm confident in your ability to do that. "Dr. Patterson asked if there was anthing else Jennifer wanted to ask or share before they closed for the day. Jennifer mentioned that she liked the meditation and wanted to know more. Dr. Patterson opened a file drawer and pulled out a few sheets of paper. On one was a list of books. She highlighted two that could be helpful. There was also a list of meditation groups and classes in the area. Dr. Patterson suggested a couple from that list that may be good places to start. Dr. Patterson added, "Having more people support you in your growth will be great in the long run. Attending a meditation group is one way you can continue to build your support system."Jennifer left Dr. Patterson's office feeling empowered about her recovery and excited that she had more tools to support her personal growth.

Epilogue

It was the last presentation for the day. Several members of the university's faculty were asked to lead seminars on their own work in psychology. About two dozen graduate students drifted into the meeting room where I would speak. As we were about to begin, to my surprise, a few of my colleagues – other faculty in the School of Social and Behavioral Sciences at Capella University — also arrived. I hadn't expected other faculty to attend this presentation on the integration of spirituality in mental health practice, but I was happy to see them.

The seminar was scheduled for 90 minutes. In that time, there was discussion of the definition of spirituality and the integrated model of the self. The session was animated as the grad students attempted to integrate the information with their experience. My faculty colleagues were quiet, took notes, but made no interjections.

At the end of the presentation, the faculty left first. Because of their lack of participation, I wondered about their impressions. I chatted with the few students who stayed after the seminar for some follow-up.

When I left the room, I found my colleagues waiting for me in a corridor. It seemed as though they began to speak at once. "I do a lot of work consulting with Christian counseling agencies. The model you presented would make a lot of sense to them. Why haven't you published anything about this model?" Another chimed in, "I've been working with women survivors of cancer for years. I focus on personal empowerment as survivors. This model would enable them to understand their experience much more clearly." In short, my colleagues were animated and supportive, conveying the concern about that the lack of a systemic, holistic approach in traditional mental health training, and enthusiastic about the relevance of this model for use in a variety of settings.

Perhaps the most important comment made by my colleagues that I've also consistently heard from other mental health professionals is that integrated approaches that address the multiple dimensions of the individual have been absent from graduate education in the mental health professions. Like me, my faculty colleagues hold Ph.D.'s, are experienced clinicians, and known for our expertise within our areas of specialization. Yet, as a group, there is recognition that despite the research evidence that supports the role of spirituality in mental health, integrated approaches to mental health are inadequately addressed. Instead, mental health practitioners today generally approach spirituality through a patch-work of tools if they address it at all.

It is my hope that mental health professionals from across specializations will use the definition of spirituality articulated in this volume as well as the integrated model of self as a foundation for further exploration toward the integration of spirituality in mental health practice. We are entering a new era in the practice of psychology in which multiple avenues in research demonstrate that something viewed as personal and intangible, spirituality, plays a significant role in mental health. The challenge for us in this era is to take something we often view as intangible and make it applicable for our clients. This is, indeed, an exciting opportunity in the evolution of psychology.

References

Anadarajah, G., & Hight, E. (2001). Spirituality and medical practice: Using the HOPE questions as a practical tool for spiritual assessment. *American Family Physician,* 63(1); 81-88.

Baetz, M., & Toews, J. (2009). Clinical implications of research on religion, spirituality, and mental health. *Canadian Journal of Psychiatry,* 54(5); 292-301.

Baylor Institute for Studies of Religion. (2006) American Piety in the 21st Century : New Insights into the Depth and Complexity of Religion in the US. Retrieved from http://www.baylor.edu/content/services/document.php/33304.pdf

Benson, H., & Klipper, M. (1975). *The Relaxation Response.* New York, NY: William Morrow and Company.

Bradshaw, M., & Ellison, C. (2008). Do genetic factors influence religious life? Findings from a behavior genetic analysis of twin siblings. Journal for the Scientific Study of Religion. 47(4); 529-544.

Comings, D., Gonzeles, N., Saucier, G., Johnson, J., & MacMurray, J. (2000) The DNR$ gene and the spiritual transcendence scale of the character temperament index. *Psychiatric Genetics,* 10(4); 185-189.

Chin, J. (2005). *Learning from my Mother's voice: Family legend and the Chinese American immigrant experience.* New York: TC Press.

Duran, E. (2006). *Healing the Soul Wound: Counseling with American Indians and Other Native Peoples.* New York, NY: Teachers College Press.

Duran, E., & Duran, B. (1995). *Native American Postcolonial Psychology.* Albany, NY: State University of New York Press.

Eaude, T. (2009). Happiness, emotional well-being and mental health – what has children's spirituality to offer? *International*

Journal of Children's Spirituality 14(3);185–196.

Fetzer Institute (2003). *Multidimensional Measurement of Religiousness/Spirituality for Use in Health Research.* Retrieved from http://www.fetzer.org/images/stories/pdf/Multidimens ionalBooklet.pdf

Fouad, N., & Arredondo, P. (2006) *Becoming Culturally Oriented: Practical Advice for Psychologists and Educators.* Washington, D.C.: American Psychological Association

Frankl, V. (1988). *The Will to Meaning: Foundations and Applications of Logotherapy.* New York, NY: Mariner Books.

Hammer, D. (2004). *The God Gene: How Faith is Hardwired into Our Genes.* New York, NY: Doubleday.

Hufford, D., Fritts, M., & Rhodes, J. (2010). Spiritual fitness. *Military Medicine*, 175:73-87.

Huxley, A. (1963) *Island.* New York, NY: Bantam Books.

Jackson, D., Firtko, A., & Edenborough, M. (2007). Personal resilience as a strategy for surviving and thriving in the face of workplace adversity: a literature review. *Journal of Advanced Nursing* 60(1); 1–9.

Kabat-Zinn, J. (2006). *Coming to our senses: healing ourselves and the world through mindfulness.* New York: Hyperion Books.

Kohls, N., Walach, H., & Wirtz, M. (2009). The relationship between spiritual experiences, transpersonal trust, social support, and sense of coherence and mental distress—a comparison of spiritually practising and non-practising samples. *Mental Health, Religion & Culture*, 12(1); 1-23.

Koenig, H. (1998) *The Handbook of Religion and Mental Health.* Maryland Heights, MO: Academic Press.

Koenig, H. (2000). Religion, spirituality, and medicine: application to clinical practice. *Journal of the American Medical Association,* 284(1) 1708-1909.

Koenig, L., McGue, M., Krueger, R. &Bouchard, T. (2005). Genetic and environmental influences of religiousness: findings for retrospective and current religiousness ratings. Journal of

Personality 73:2, 471-488.

Kapogiannis, D., Barbey, A., Su, M., Zamboni, G., Kruegger, K, & Grafman, J. (2009). Cognitive and neural foundations of religious belief. Proceedings of the National Academy of Sciences 106(12); 4876-4881.

Langer, N. (2004). Resiliency and spirituality: foundations of strengths perspective counseling with the elderly. *Educational Gerontology*, 30: 611–617.

Lo B., Quill T., & Tulsky J. (1999) Discussing palliative care with patients. *Annals of Internal Medicine.* 130:744-749.

Lukoff, D. (2007). Spirituality in the recovery from persistent mental disorders. *Southern Medical Journal,* 100(6); 642-646.

Maugan, T. (1996). The SPIRITual history. *Archives of Family Medicine,* 5:11-16.

Newberg, A., & Waldman, M. (2009). *How God Changes Your Brain,* New York, NY: Ballantine Books.

Parham, T., Ajamu, A., & White, J. (2010). *Psychology of Blacks: Center Our Perspectives in the African Consciousness,* Fourth Edition. Upper Saddle River, NJ: Prentice Hall.

Rogers, C. (1995). *On Becoming a Person: A Therapists View of Psychotherapy.* New York, NY: Mariner Books.

Peres, J., Moriera-Almeida, A., Nazella, A, & Hoenig, H. (2007). Spirituality and resilience in trauma victims. *Journal of Religion and Health,* 46:343-350.

Sorajjkool, S., Aja, V., Chilson, B., Ramirez-Johnson, J., & Earll, A. (2008). Disconnection, depression, and spirituality: a study of the role of spirituality and meaning in the lives of individuals with severe depression, *Pastoral Psychology,* 56:521-532.

Sossou, M., Craig, C., Ogren, H. & Schnak, M. (2008). A qualitative study of resilience factors of Bosnian refugee women resettled in the Southern United States. *Journal of Ethnic and Cultural Diversity in Social Work,* 17(4); 365-385.

Sue, D., & Sue, D., (2007) *Counseling the culturally diverse: theory and practice,* fifth edition. Hobohen, NJ: Wiley Press.

Van Der Poel, C. (1998) *Sharing the Journey: Spiritual Assessment and Pastoral Response to Persons with Incurable Illnesses.* Collegeville, MN: Liturgical Press.

Van Dyke, C., Glenwick, D., Cecero, J., & Kim, S. (2009). The relationship of religious coping and spirituality to adjustment and psychological distress in urban early adolescents. *Mental Health, Religion and Culture.* 12(4); 369-383.

Van Kaam, A. (1983). Formative Spirituality, Volume One: Foundational Formation. New York, NY: Crossroad Publishing Company.

Vygostsky, L. (1978). *Mind in Society: The Development of Higher Psychological Processes.* Cambridge, MA: Harvard University Press.

About the Author

The Rev. Dr. Louis F. Kavar is an experienced therapist, spiritual director, minster, and professor of psychology. Throughout his career, Dr. Kavar has worked with individuals, groups and organizations in area of spirituality. He has led retreats, taught classes, and presented seminars throughout the United States, Canada, Mexico, England, Australia, and New Zealand. His relaxed manner and use of humor make him an exceptional and accessible presenter in the area of spirituality.

An ordained minister in the United Church of Christ, Dr. Kavar brings over thirty years of experience in working with individuals and groups in the areas of personal and spiritual development. Dr. Kavar teaches in the doctoral program in psychology at the Harold Abel School of Social and Behavorial Sciences in Capella University.

Dr. Kavar previously lived in Tucson, AZ where he was the director of Desert Vision Counseling and Hypnotherapy, a private practice specializing in issues of spirituality, wholeness and creativity. He was also among the faculty and design team for the Hesychia School of Spiritual Direction.

Having also been a resident of Miami, Dr. Kavar was the clinical director for South Florida's Pastoral Care Network. Headquartered at the United Protestant Appeal, this program provided spiritually based counseling to people living with chronic illnesses and their loved ones in a three county region. He was also preceptor for spiritual care in a residency program at the University of Miami's Department of Psychiatry.

Kavar holds the degrees of Master of Arts in spirituality from the Institute of Formative Spirituality at Duquesne University, and a Doctor of Philosophy in counseling from the School of Education at the University of Pittsburgh. He is also a Nationally Certified Psychologist credentialed by the National Board of

Professional Psychologist, a hypnotherapist by the National Guild of Hypnotists and an addictions counselor by the National Board of Addiction Examiners. Kavar currently resides in Atlanta, GA with his partner, Kin and his tuxedo cat, Kedvesh.

B O O K S

O is a symbol of the world, of oneness and unity. In different cultures it also means the "eye," symbolizing knowledge and insight. We aim to publish books that are accessible, constructive and that challenge accepted opinion, both that of academia and the "moral majority."

Our books are available in all good English language bookstores worldwide. If you don't see the book on the shelves ask the bookstore to order it for you, quoting the ISBN number and title. Alternatively you can order online (all major online retail sites carry our titles) or contact the distributor in the relevant country, listed on the copyright page.

See our website **www.o-books.net** for a full list of over 500 titles, growing by 100 a year.

And tune in to myspiritradio.com for our book review radio show, hosted by June-Elleni Laine, where you can listen to the authors discussing their books.

mySpiritRadio